Modern Control Systems Analysis and Design Using MATLAB®

Robert H. Bishop
The University of Texas at Austin

ADDISON-WESLEY PUBLISHING COMPANY
Reading, Massachusetts • Menlo Park, California • New York
Don Mills, Ontario • Wokingham, England • Amsterdam • Bonn
Sydney • Singapore • Tokyo • Madrid • San Juan • Milan • Paris

MATLAB is a registered trademark of The Mathworks, Inc.

Bishop, Robert H. , 1957–
    Modern control systems : analysis and design using MATLAB / Robert
H. Bishop.
        p.   cm.
    ISBN 0-201-59657-1
    1. Automatic control--Data processing. 2. MATLAB. 3. System
design.   I. Title.
TJ213.B5357 1993
629.8'3--dc20
                                                            92–21127
                                                                CIP

Reproduced by Addison-Wesley from camera-ready copy supplied
by the author.

1 2 3 4 5 6 7 8 9 10-AL-96959493

For

Robert Emerson

and

Joseph Taylor

Preface

This book is designed as a companion text to the Sixth Edition of *Modern Control Systems* by Richard C. Dorf. The objective is to supplement the classical and modern control theory presented in Dorf's book with an introduction to control system design and analysis using *MATLAB*.

The basic structure of the text is similar to *Modern Control Systems* (abbreviated throughout as *MCS*). The main difference lies in the first chapter. We begin with an introduction to *MATLAB*, whereas *MCS* begins with an introduction to control systems. The remaining chapters follow the general structure found in *MCS*. Since many *MATLAB* functions are defined in the chapters following the first chapter, the text is meant to be read in chronological order.

To properly utilize this text it is essential to have access to *MCS*. Many of the illustrative problems and design examples in Dorf's book are solved here using *MATLAB*, but in some cases the background information and problem motivation presented in *MCS* is not duplicated here.

It is assumed that the student has access to *MATLAB* and the *Control System Toolbox*. All of the *MATLAB* examples contained herein were developed and tested on a Macintosh IIfx with the full version of *MATLAB* and the *Control System Toolbox*. A complete test of all the scripts was also conducted on an IBM AT with good results. Since it is not possible to verify each example on all the available computer platforms that are compatible with *MATLAB*, an attempt was made to restrict the *MATLAB* topics covered in this book to those that are computer-platform independent. It might be very helpful to have access to a *MATLAB Users Guide*.

I wish to express my appreciation to Professor Richard C. Dorf for his guidance throughout the development of this text. I also would like to thank Brian L. Jones and P. Daniel Burkhart for their reviews of the final manuscript.

Finally, my deep gratitude goes to my wife, Lynda, for assisting in typing the manuscript and for her continuous support and encouragement.

R.H.B.

Austin, Texas

Contents

Chapter 1

MATLAB Basics

1.1   Introduction

MATLAB is an interactive program for scientific and engineering calculations. The *MATLAB* family of programs includes the base program plus a variety of *toolboxes*. The toolboxes are a collection of special files, called *M-files*, which extend the functionality of the base program. Together the base program plus the *Control System Toolbox* provide the capability to use *MATLAB* for control system design and analysis. In the remainder of this book, whenever we refer to *MATLAB*, you can interpret that as meaning the base program plus the *Control System Toolbox*.

Most of the statements, functions, and commands are computer platform *independent*. Regardless of what particular computer system you use, your interaction with *MATLAB* is basically the same. This book concentrates on this computer platform independent interaction. A typical *session* will utilize a variety of objects that allow you to interact with the program. These objects are

1. statements and variables,

2. matrices,

3. graphics, and

4. scripts.

1

MATLAB interprets and acts on input in the form of one or more of these objects. Our goal in this chapter is to introduce each of the four objects in preparation for our ultimate goal of using *MATLAB* for control system design and analysis.

The manner in which *MATLAB* interacts with your computer system is computer platform *dependent*. Examples of computer dependent functions include installation, the file structure, generating hardcopies of the graphics, invoking and exiting a session, and memory allocation. Questions related to platform dependent issues are not addressed here. This is not to imply that they are not important, but rather that there are better sources of information such as your *Users Guide* and your local resident expert. This book is **not** intended as a substitute for your *Users Guide*.

Before proceeding, make sure that you can invoke a session and exit *MATLAB* . You need to be able to get to the command window and see the command prompt " >> ". To begin a session on a Macintosh you will probably double-click on the *MATLAB* program icon. On an IBM PC compatible you will probably type **matlab** at the DOS prompt.

The remainder of this chapter is organized as follows. There are four sections corresponding to the four objects listed above. In the first section we present the basics of *statements and variables*. Following that is the subject of *matrices*. The third section presents an introduction to *graphics*, and the chapter concludes with a discussion on the important topic of *scripts* and *M-files*.

1.2   Statements and Variables

Statements have the form shown in Figure 1.1. *MATLAB* uses the assignment so that equals ("=") implies the assignment of the expression to the variable. The command prompt is two right arrows, " >> ". A *typical* statement is shown in Figure 1.2, wherein we are entering a 2×2 matrix to which we attach the variable name A. The statement is executed after the carriage return (or enter key) is pressed. The carriage return is not explicitly denoted in the remaining examples in this and subsequent chapters.

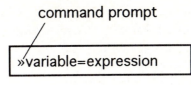

Figure 1.1 *MATLAB* Statement Form.

The matrix **A** is automatically displayed after the statement is executed following the carriage return. If the statement is followed by a semicolon (;), the output matrix **A** is suppressed, as seen in Figure 1.3. The assignment of the variable **A** has been carried out even though the output is suppressed by the semicolon. It is often the case that your *MATLAB* sessions will include intermediate calculations for which the output is of little interest. You should use the semicolon whenever you have a need to reduce the amount of output. Output management has the added benefit of increasing the execution speed of the calculations, since displaying screen output takes time.

The usual mathematical operators can be used in expressions. The common operators are shown in Table 1.1. The order of the arithmetic operations can be altered by using parentheses.

The example in Figure 1.4 illustrates that *MATLAB* can be used in a "calculator" mode. When the variable name and "=" are omitted from an expression, the result is assigned to the generic variable *ans*. *MATLAB* has available most of the trigonometric and elementary math functions of a common scientific calculator. The *Users*

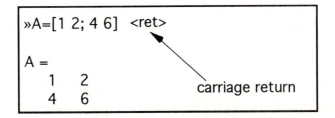

Figure 1.2 Example Statement: Matrix Input.

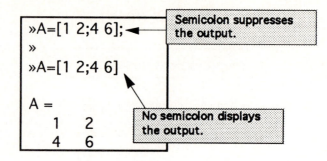

Figure 1.3 Using Semicolons to Suppress the Output.

Guide has a complete list of available trigonometric and elementary math functions; the more common ones are summarized in Table 1.2.

Variable names begin with a letter and are followed by any number of letters and numbers (including underscores). Keep the name length to 19 characters since *MATLAB* remembers only the first 19 characters. It is a good practice to use variable names that describe the quantity they represent. For example, we might use the variable name *vel* to represent the quantity *aircraft velocity*. Generally, we do not use extremely long variable names even though they may be legal *MATLAB* names.

Since *MATLAB* is *case sensitive*, the variables M and m are not the same variables. By *case* we mean upper and lower case. This is illustrated in Figure 1.5. The variables M and m are recognized as different quantities.

Table 1.1 Mathematical Operators.

+	Addition
-	Subtraction
*	Multiplication
/	Division
^	Power

```
»12.4/6.9

ans =
     1.7971
```

Figure 1.4 Calculator Mode.

MATLAB has several predefined variables, including *pi, Inf, Nan, i*, and *j*. Three examples are shown in Figure 1.6. *Nan* stands for *Not-a-Number* and results from undefined operations. *Inf* represents $+\infty$ and *pi* represents π. The variable $i = \sqrt{-1}$ is used to represent complex numbers. The variable $j = \sqrt{-1}$ can be used for

Table 1.2 Common Mathematical Functions.

sin(X)	Sine of the elements of X
cos(X)	Cosine of the elements of X
asin(X)	Arcsine of the elements of X
acos(X)	Arccosine of the elements of X
tan(X)	Tangent of the elements of X
atan(X)	Arctangent of the elements of X
atan2(X,Y)	Four quadrant arctangent of the real elements of X and Y
abs(X)	Absolute value of the elements of X
sqrt(X)	Square root of X
imag(X)	Imaginary part of X
real(X)	Real part of X
conj(X)	Complex conjugate of X
log(X)	Natural logarithm of the elements of X
log10(X)	Logarithm base 10 of the elements of X
exp(X)	Exponential of the elements of X

```
»M=[1 2];
»m=[3 5 7];
```

Figure 1.5 Variables Are Case Sensitive.

complex arithmetic by those who prefer it over i. These predefined variables can be inadvertently overwritten. Of course, they can also be purposely overwritten in order to free up the variable name for other uses. For instance, one might want to use i as an integer and reserve j for complex arithmetic. Be safe and leave these predefined variables alone, as there are plenty of alternative names that can be used. Predefined variables can be reset to their default values by using **clear** *name* (e.g., **clear** *pi*).

The matrix $\boldsymbol{A}$ and the variable *ans*, in Figures 1.3 and 1.4, are stored in the *workspace*. Variables in the workspace are automati-

```
»z=3+4*i

z =
        3.0000 + 4.0000i

»Inf

ans =
        ∞

»0/0

Warning: Divide by zero
ans =
        NaN
```

Figure 1.6 Three Predefined Variables i, *Inf*, and *Nan*.

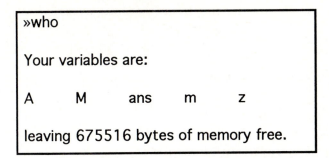

Figure 1.7 Using the **who** Function to Display Variables.

cally saved for later use in your session. The **who** function gives a list of the variables in the workspace, as shown in Figure 1.7.

MATLAB has a host of built-in functions. You can refer to the *Users Guide* for a complete list. We will describe each function we use as the need arises.

The **whos** function lists the variables in the workspace and gives additional information regarding variable dimension, type, and memory allocation. Figure 1.8 gives an example of the **whos** function.

The memory allocation information given by the **whos** function can be interpreted as follows. Each element of the 2×2 matrix A

```
»whos
        Name      Size       Total     Complex

         A       2 by 2        4        No
         M       1 by 2        2        No
        ans      1 by 1        1        No
         m       1 by 3        3        No
         z       1 by 1        2        Yes

Grand total is (12 * 8) = 96 bytes,
leaving 664912 bytes of memory free.
```

Figure 1.8 Using the **whos** Function to Display Variables.

```
»clear A
»who

Your variables are:

M        ans      m       z

leaving 663780 bytes of memory free.
```

Figure 1.9 Removing the Matrix *A* from the Workspace.

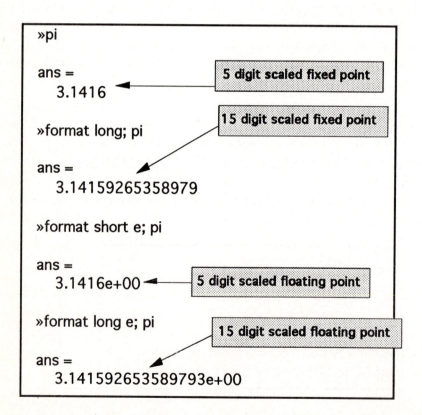

Figure 1.10 Output Format Control Illustrates the Four Forms of the Output.

requires 8 bytes of memory for a total of 32 bytes, the 1×1 variable *ans* requires 8 bytes, and so forth. All the variables in the workspace are using a total of 96 bytes. The amount of remaining free memory depends upon the total memory available in the system. Computers with virtual memory will not display the remaining free memory.

You can remove variables from the workspace with the **clear** function. Using the function **clear**, by itself, removes all items (variables and functions) from the workspace; **clear variables** removes all variables from the workspace; **clear** *name1 name 2 ...* removes the variables *name1, name2*, and so forth. The procedure for removing the matrix **A** from the workspace is shown in Figure 1.9.

A simple calculation shows that clearing the matrix **A** from memory freed up more than 32 bytes. In some cases, clearing a variable may not change the value of the displayed free memory at all. The **who** function displays the amount of *contiguous* remaining free memory. So, depending upon the "location" of the variable in the workspace, clearing the variable may or may not increase the displayed amount of remaining free memory. The point is that your available free memory may be more than displayed with the **who** or **whos** functions.

All computations in *MATLAB* are performed in *double precision*. However, the screen output can be displayed in several formats. The default output format contains four digits past the decimal point for nonintegers. This can be changed by using the **format** function shown in Figure 1.10. Once a particular format has been specified, it remains in effect until altered by a different **format** input.

```
» WHO
??? Undefined function or variable
Symbol in question ==> WHO

» Who
??? Undefined function or variable
Symbol in question ==> Who
```

Figure 1.11 Function Names are Case Sensitive.

Remember that the output format does not affect the *MATLAB* computations — all computations are in double precision.

On the other hand, the number of digits displayed does not necessarily reflect the number of significant digits of the number. This is problem dependent, and only you can know the true accuracy of the numbers that you input and that *MATLAB* displays.

Since *MATLAB* is case sensitive, the functions **who** and **WHO** are not the same functions. The function **who** is a built-in function, so typing **who** lists the variables in the workspace. On the other hand, typing the uppercase **WHO** results in the error message shown in Figure 1.11. Case sensitivity applies to all functions.

1.3   Matrices

MATLAB is short for *matrix laboratory*. The *Users Guide* describes the program as a high-performance interactive software package designed to provide easy access to the *LINPACK* and *EISPACK* matrix software. Although we will not dwell on the matrix routines underlying our calculations, we will learn how to use the interactive capability to assist us in our control system design and analysis. We begin by introducing the basic concepts associated with manipulating matrices and vectors.

The basic computational unit is the matrix. Vectors and scalars can be viewed as special cases of matrices. A typical matrix expression is enclosed in square brackets, [·]. The column elements are separated by blanks or commas and the rows are separated by semicolons or carriage returns. Suppose we want to input the matrix A, where

$$A = \begin{bmatrix} 1 & -4j & \sqrt{2} \\ \log(-1) & \sin(\pi/2) & \cos(\pi/3) \\ \arcsin(0.5) & \arccos(0.8) & \exp(0.8) \end{bmatrix}.$$

One way to input A is shown in Figure 1.12. The input style in Figure 1.12 is not unique.

Matrices can be input across multiple lines by using a carriage return following the semicolon or in place of the semicolon. This is useful for entering large matrices. Different combinations of spaces

```
»A=[1, -4*j, sqrt(2);          3 x 3 complex matrix
log(-1)  sin(pi/2)  cos(pi/3)
asin(0.5),  acos(0.8)  exp(0.8)]


A =
   1.0000              0 - 4.0000i  1.4142
           0 + 3.1416i  1.0000        0.5000
   0.5236             0.6435         2.2255


»A=[1 2;4 5]                2 x 2 real matrix


A =
    1    2
    4    5
```

Figure 1.12 Complex and Real Matrix Input with Automatic Dimension and Type Adjustment.

and commas can be used to separate the columns, and different combinations of semicolons and carriage returns can be used to separate the rows, as illustrated in Figure 1.12.

No dimension statements or type statements are necessary when using matrices; memory is allocated automatically. Notice in the example in Figure 1.12 that the size of the matrix A is automatically adjusted when the input matrix is redefined. Also notice that the matrix elements can contain trigonometric and elementary math functions, as well as complex numbers.

The important basic matrix operations are addition and subtraction, multiplication, transpose, powers, and the so-called array operations, which are element-to-element operations. The mathematical operators given in Table 1.1 apply to matrices. We will not discuss *matrix division*, but be aware that *MATLAB* has a left- and right-matrix division capability.

Matrix operations require that the matrix dimensions be *compatible*. For matrix addition and subtraction this means that the matrices must have the same dimensions. If A is an $n \times m$ matrix and B is a $p \times r$ matrix, then $A \pm B$ is permitted only if $n = p$ and $m = r$. Matrix multiplication, given by $A * B$, is permitted only if $m = p$. Matrix-vector multiplication is a special case of matrix multiplication. Suppose b is a vector of length p. Multiplication of the vector b by the matrix A, where A is an $n \times m$ matrix, is allowed if $m = p$. Thus, $y = A * b$ is the $n \times 1$ vector solution of $A * b$. Examples of three basic matrix-vector operations are given in Figure 1.13.

The matrix transpose is formed with the apostrophe ('). We can use the matrix transpose and multiplication operation to create a vector *inner product* in the following manner. Suppose w and v are $m \times 1$ vectors. Then the inner product (also known as the dot

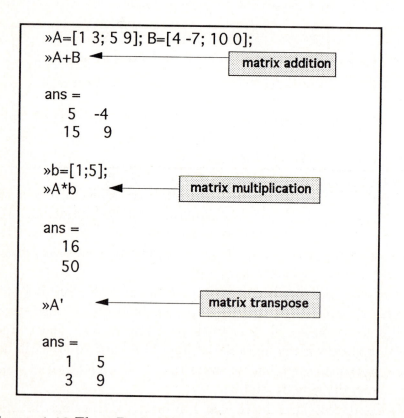

Figure 1.13 Three Basic Matrix Operations: Addition, Multiplication, and Transpose.

product) is given by $\boldsymbol{w}' * \boldsymbol{v}$. The inner product of two vectors is a scalar. The *outer product* of two vectors can similarly be computed as $\boldsymbol{w} * \boldsymbol{v}'$. The outer product of two $m \times 1$ vectors is an $m \times m$ matrix of rank 1. Examples of inner and outer products are given in Figure 1.14.

The basic matrix operations can be modified for element-by-element operations by preceding the operator with a period. The modified matrix operations are known as *array operations*. The commonly used array operators are given in Table 1.3. Matrix addition and subtraction are already element-by-element operations and do not require the additional period preceding the operator. However, array multiplication, division, and power do require the preceding dot, as shown in Table 1.3.

Suppose A and B are 2×2 matrices given by

$$A = \begin{bmatrix} a_{11} & a_{12} \\ a_{21} & a_{22} \end{bmatrix} \quad , \quad B = \begin{bmatrix} b_{11} & b_{12} \\ b_{21} & b_{22} \end{bmatrix}.$$

Then, using the array multiplication operator, we have

$$A .* B = \begin{bmatrix} a_{11}b_{11} & a_{12}b_{12} \\ a_{21}b_{21} & a_{22}b_{22} \end{bmatrix}.$$

```
»x=[5;pi;sin(pi/2)]; y=[exp(-0.5);-13;pi^2];
»x'*y                                              inner product

ans =
    -27.9384

»x*y'                                              outer product

ans =
     3.0327  -65.0000  49.3480
     1.9055  -40.8407  31.0063
     0.6065  -13.0000   9.8696
```

Figure 1.14 Inner and Outer Products.

Table 1.3 Mathematical Array Operators.

+	Addition
-	Subtraction
.*	Multiplication
./	Division
.^	Power

The elements of $A.*B$ are the products of the corresponding elements of A and B. A numerical example of two array operations is given in Figure 1.15.

Before proceeding to the important topic of *graphics*, we need to introduce the notion of *subscripting* using *colon notation*. The colon notation, shown in Figure 1.16, allows us to generate a row vector containing the numbers from a given starting value, x_i, to a final value, x_f, with a specified increment, dx.

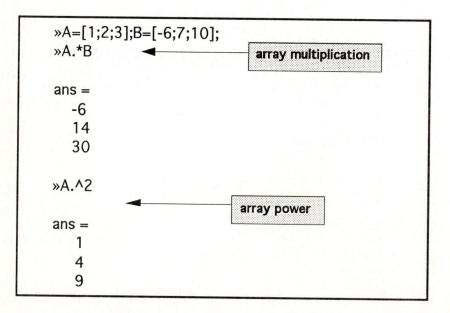

Figure 1.15 Array Operations.

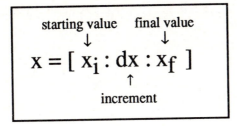

Figure 1.16 The Colon Notation.

We can easily generate vectors using the colon notation, and as we shall soon see, this is quite useful for developing *x-y plots*. Suppose our objective is to generate a plot of $y = x\sin(x)$ versus x for $x = 0, 0.1, 0.2, \ldots, 1.0$. Our first step is to generate a table of *x-y* data. We can generate a vector containing the values of x at which the values of $y(x)$ are desired using the colon notation. This is illustrated in Figure 1.17. Given the desired x vector, the vector

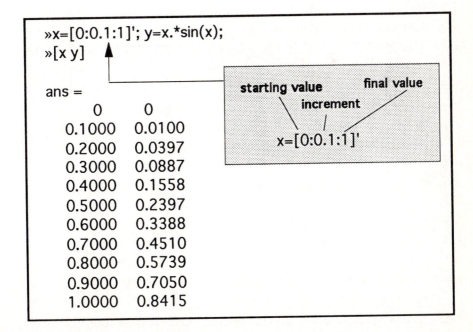

Figure 1.17 Generating Vectors Using the Colon Notation.

$y(x)$ is computed using the multiplication array operation. Creating a plot of $y = x\sin(x)$ versus x is a simple step once the table of x-y data is generated.

1.4   Graphics

Graphics play an important role in both the design and analysis of control systems. An important component of an *interactive* control system design and analysis tool is an effective graphical capability. A complete solution to the control system design and analysis will eventually require a detailed look at a multitude of data types in many formats. The important plot formats include root-locus plots, Bode plots, Nyquist plots, and time-response plots. The objective of this section is to acquaint the reader with the basic x-y plotting capability of *MATLAB* . More advanced graphics topics are addressed as the need arises.

MATLAB uses a *graph display* to present plots. Some computer configurations allow both the command display and graph display to be viewed simultaneously. On computer configurations that allow only one to be viewed at a time, the command display will disappear when the graph display is up. The graph display is brought up automatically when a plot is generated using any function which generates a plot (e.g., the **plot** function). Switching from the graph display back to the command display is accomplished by pressing any key on the keyboard. The plot in the graph display is cleared by the **clg** function at the command prompt. The **shg** function is used to switch to the graph display from the command display.

There are two basic groups of graphics functions. The first group of functions, shown in Table 1.4, specifies the type of plot. The list of available plot types includes x-y plot, semilog and log plots. The second group of functions, shown in Table 1.5, allows us to customize the plots by adding titles, axis labels, and text to the plots and to change the scales and display multiple plots in subwindows.

The standard x-y plot is created using the **plot** function. The x-y data in Figure 1.17 are plotted using the **plot** function as shown

Table 1.4 Available Plot Formats.

plot(x,y)	Plots the vector x versus the vector y.
semilogx(x,y)	Plots the vector x versus the vector y. The x-axis is $\log_{10}$; the y axis is linear.
semilogy(x,y)	Plots the vector x versus the vector y. The x-axis is linear; the y axis is $\log_{10}$.
loglog(x,y)	Plots the vector x versus the vector y. Creates a plot with $\log_{10}$ scales on both axes.

in Figure 1.18. The axis scales and line types are automatically chosen. The axes are labeled with the **xlabel** and **ylabel** commands; the title is applied with the **title** command. A grid can be placed on the plot by using the **grid** command. We see that a basic x-y plot is generated with the combination of functions **plot, xlabel, ylabel, title,** and **grid**.

Multiple lines can be placed on the graph by using the **plot** function with multiple arguments, as shown in Figure 1.19. The default

Table 1.5 Functions for Customized Plots.

title('text')	Puts 'text' at the top of the plot.
xlabel('text')	Labels the x-axis with 'text'.
ylabel('text')	Labels the y-axis with 'text'.
text(p1,p2,'text','sc')	Puts 'text' at (p1,p2) in screen coordinates where (0.0,0.0) is the lower left and (1.0,1.0) is the upper right of the screen.
subplot	Subdivides the graphics window.
grid	Draws grid lines on the current plot.

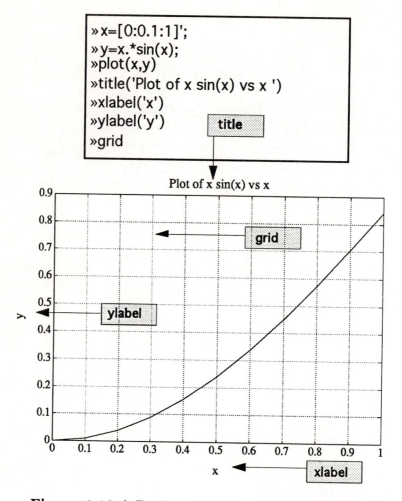

Figure 1.18 A Basic x-y Plot of $x\sin(x)$ versus x.

line types can also be altered. The available line types are shown in Table 1.6. The line types will be automatically chosen unless specified by the user. The use of the **text** function and changing the line types is illustrated in Figure 1.19.

The other graphics functions **loglog**, **semilogx**, and **semilogy** are used in a similar fashion to **plot**. To obtain an x-y plot where the x-axis is a linear scale and the y-axis is a $\log_{10}$ scale, you would use the **semilogy** function in place of the **plot** function. The cus-

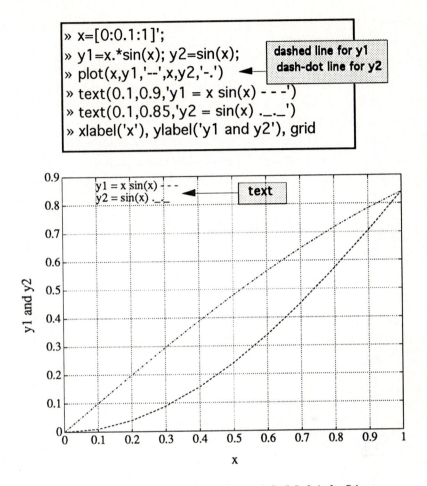

```
» x=[0:0.1:1]';
» y1=x.*sin(x); y2=sin(x);
» plot(x,y1,'--',x,y2,'-.')        dashed line for y1
» text(0.1,0.9,'y1 = x sin(x) - - -')   dash-dot line for y2
» text(0.1,0.85,'y2 = sin(x) ._._')
» xlabel('x'), ylabel('y1 and y2'), grid
```

Figure 1.19 A Basic *x-y* Plot with Multiple Lines.

Table 1.6 Line Types for Customized Plots.

-	Solid line
- -	Dashed line
:	Dotted line
-.	Dashdot line

tomizing features listed in Table 1.5 can also be utilized with the
loglog, **semilogx**, and **semilogy** functions.

The graph display can be subdivided into smaller subwindows.
The function **subplot**(mnp) subdivides the graph display into an
$m \times n$ grid of smaller subwindows, where $m \leq 2$ and $n \leq 2$. This
means the *graph display* can be subdivided into two or four windows.
The integer p specifies the window, where the windows are numbered
left to right, top to bottom. This is illustrated in Figure 1.20, where
the graphics window is subdivided into four subwindows.

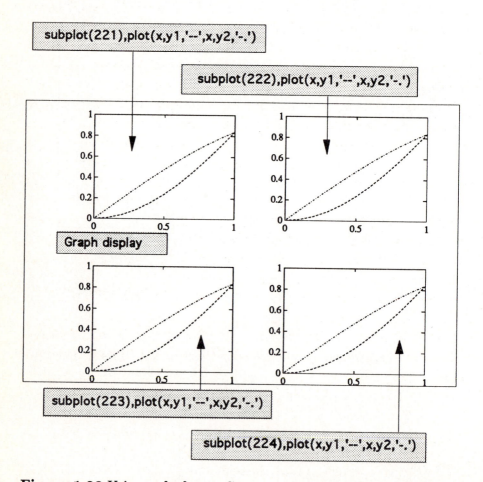

Figure 1.20 Using **subplot** to Create a 2×2 Partition of the Graph
Display.

1.5 Scripts

Up to this point, all of our interaction with *MATLAB* has been at the command prompt. We enter statements and functions at the command prompt, and *MATLAB* interprets our input and takes the appropriate action. This is the preferable mode of operation whenever your sessions are short and nonrepetitive. However, the real power of *MATLAB* for control system design and analysis derives from its ability to execute a long sequence of commands stored in a file. These files are called *M-files* since the filename has the form *filename.m*. A *script* is one type of *M-file*. The *Control System Toolbox* is a collection of *M-files* designed specifically for control applications. In addition to the pre-existing *M-files* delivered with *MATLAB* and the toolboxes, we can develop *scripts* for our applications.

Scripts are ordinary ASCII text files and are created by using your own text editor. Creating and storing *scripts* are computer platform dependent topics, which means that you need to seek out the appropriate expert at your location for more information.

A *script* is just a sequence of ordinary statements and functions that you would use at the command prompt level. A *script* is invoked at the command prompt level by simply typing in the filename (without the .m file type). *Scripts* can also invoke other *scripts*. When the *script* is invoked, *MATLAB* executes the statements and functions in the file without waiting for input at the command prompt. The *script* operates on variables in the workspace.

Suppose we want to plot the function $y(t) = \sin \alpha t$, where α is a variable that we want to vary. Using our favorite text editor, we write a *script*, which we will call **plotdata.m**. This is shown in Figure 1.21. We input a value of α at the command prompt, and in doing so we place α in the workspace. Then we execute the script by typing in **plotdata** at the command prompt. The script **plotdata.m** will use the most recent value of α in the workspace. After executing the script we can enter another value of α at the command prompt and execute the script again.

Your *scripts* should be well documented with *comments*. A comment begins with a %. If you put a *header* in your *script* comprised of several descriptive comments regarding the function of the *script*,

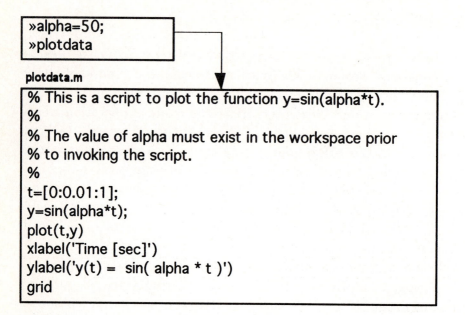

Figure 1.21 A Simple *Script* to Plot the Function $y(t) = \sin \alpha t$.

then using the **help** function will display the header comments and describe the script to the user. This is illustrated in Figure 1.22.

We use **plotdata.m** to develop an interactive capability with α as a variable, as shown in Figure 1.23. At the command prompt, we input a value of $\alpha = 10$ followed by the *script* filename, which in this case is **plotdata**. The graph of $y(t) = \sin \alpha t$ is automatically

```
»help plotdata

This is a script to plot the function y=sin(alpha*t).

The value of alpha must exist in the workspace prior
to invoking the script.
```

Figure 1.22 Using the **help** Function.

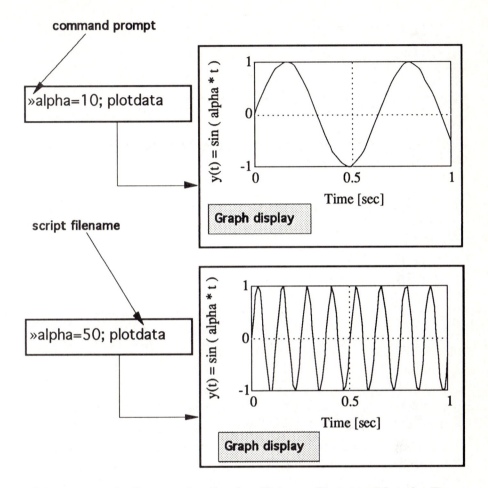

Figure 1.23 An Interactive Session Using a *Script* to Plot the Function $y(t) = \sin \alpha t$.

generated. We can now go back to the command prompt, enter a value of $\alpha = 50$, and run the *script* again to obtain the updated plot.

The graphics capability of *MATLAB* extends beyond the introductory material presented here. We will investigate the issue of graphics further on an as-needed basis.

_____ Notes _____

Chapter 2

Mathematical Modeling
of Systems

2.1   Introduction

The design and analysis of control systems is based on mathematical models of complex physical systems. The mathematical models, which follow from the physical laws of the process, are generally highly coupled nonlinear differential equations. Fortunately, many physical systems behave linearly around an operating point within some range of the variables and it is possible to develop linear approximations to the physical systems. A *Taylor series* expansion is generally utilized in the linearization process. The linear approximation to the physical system is described by a linear, constant coefficient ordinary differential equation. The *Laplace transform* method is one way to compute the solution of the differential equation. The Laplace transform can also be used to obtain an input-output description of the linear, time-invariant (LTI) system in the form of a transfer function. The application of the many "classical" and "modern" control system design and analysis tools are based on LTI mathematical models. *MATLAB* can be used with LTI systems given in the form of transfer function descriptions or state-space descriptions (see Chapter 9, State-Space Methods).

We begin this chapter by showing how to use *MATLAB* to assist in the analysis of a typical spring-mass-damper mathematical model of a mechanical system. Using a *MATLAB* script, we will develop an interactive analysis capability to analyze the effects of natural frequency and damping on the unforced response of the mass displacement. This analysis will utilize the fact that we have an analytic solution that describes the unforced time response of the mass displacement.

In the subsequent sections, we will discuss transfer functions and block diagrams. In particular, we are interested in how *MATLAB* can assist us in manipulating polynomials, computing poles and zeros of transfer functions, computing closed-loop transfer functions, block diagram reduction, and computing the response of a system to a unit step input. The chapter concludes with the electric traction motor control design example found in *MCS, pp. 79-81*.

The functions covered in this chapter are **roots, roots1, series, parallel, feedback, cloop, poly, conv, polyval, printsys, minreal, pzmap,** and **step.**

2.2   Spring-Mass-Damper System

A spring-mass-damper mechanical system is shown in Figure 2.1. The motion of the mass, denoted by $y(t)$, is described by the differential equation

$$M\ddot{y}(t) + f\dot{x}(t) + Ky(t) = r(t). \tag{2.1}$$

This system is described in *MCS, pp. 36-41*. The solution, $y(t)$, of the differential equation describes the displacement of the mass as a function of time. The forcing function is represented by $r(t)$. The derivation of the spring-mass-damper mathematical model is based on the use of *ideal* springs and dampers. These ideal models for the spring and damper are based on lumped, linear, dynamic elements and only approximate the actual elements. The spring-mass-damper model, given in Eq. (2.1), is a linear, time-invariant approximation to the physical process; it is valid only in regions where the spring force is a linear function of the mass displacement and the damping due to friction is a linear function of the velocity.

The mathematical model, given in Eq. (2.1), might represent an off-road vehicle shock absorber. Our objective could be to design an active control system to make the ride smoother when traversing

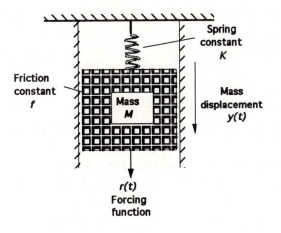

Figure 2.1 Spring-Mass-Damper System.

unpaved roads. The control design and subsequent analysis would be based on the vehicle shock absorber model in Eq. (2.1). Of course, the true test of the control design is the road test. Only then can we prove that the control design does in fact meet the objective of a smoother ride on a bumpy road. We will soon see how to use *MATLAB* to enhance our control design and analysis capability.

Many physical processes are described by mathematical models *analogous* to Eq. (2.1). A typical electrical RLC circuit is described by an analogous mathematical model where the velocity, $\dot{y}(t)$, and the voltage, $v(t)$, are analogous variables. This notion of *analogous* systems is important in system modeling. Any experience gained in designing and analyzing control systems for mechanical systems described by Eq. (2.1) can be used in controlling analogous electrical, thermal, and fluid systems.

The unforced dynamic response, $y(t)$, of the spring-mass-damper mechanical system is

$$y(t) = \frac{y(0)}{\sqrt{1-\zeta^2}}\ e^{-\zeta\omega_n t}\sin(\omega_n\sqrt{1-\zeta^2}\ t + \theta), \qquad (2.2)$$

where $\theta = \cos^{-1}\zeta$. The initial displacement is $y(0)$. The transient system response is *underdamped* when $\zeta < 1$, *overdamped* when

$\zeta > 1$, and *critically damped* when $\zeta = 1$. We can use *MATLAB* to visualize the unforced time response of the mass displacement following an initial displacement of $y(0)$. Consider the *overdamped* and *underdamped* cases:

- Case 1: $y(0)=0.15$m, $\omega_n = \sqrt{2}\frac{\text{rad}}{\text{sec}}$, $\zeta_1 = \frac{3}{2\sqrt{2}}$ $\quad(\frac{K}{M}=2, \frac{f}{M}=3)$

- Case 2: $y(0)=0.15$m, $\omega_n = \sqrt{2}\frac{\text{rad}}{\text{sec}}$, $\zeta_2 = \frac{1}{2\sqrt{2}}$ $\quad(\frac{K}{M}=2, \frac{f}{M}=1)$

The *MATLAB* commands to generate the plot of the unforced response are shown in Figure 2.2. In the *MATLAB* setup, the variables

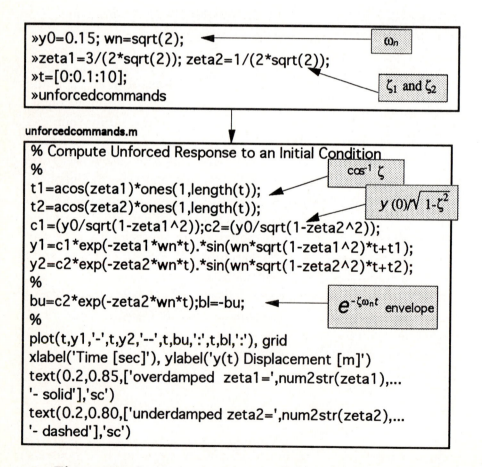

Figure 2.2 Script to Analyze the Spring-Mass-Damper.

$y(0), \omega_n, t, \zeta_1$, and ζ_2 are input to the workspace at the command level. Then the *script* **unforcedcommands.m** is executed to generate the desired plots. This creates an interactive analysis capability to analyze the effects of natural frequency and damping on the unforced response of the mass displacement. You can investigate the effects of the natural frequency and the damping on the time response by simply entering new values of ω_n, ζ_1, or ζ_2 at the command prompt and running the script **unforcedcommands.m** again. The time-response plot is in Figure 2.3. Notice that the script automatically labels the plot with the values of the damping coefficients. This avoids confusion when making many interactive simulations. The natural frequency value could also be automatically labeled on the plot. Utilizing scripts is an important aspect of developing an effective interactive design and analysis capability in *MATLAB*. Since you can relate the natural frequency and damping to the spring constant, K, and friction, f, you can also analyze the effects of K and f on the response.

In the spring-mass-damper problem, the unforced solution to the differential equation, given in Eq. (2.1), was readily available. In general, when simulating closed-loop feedback control systems

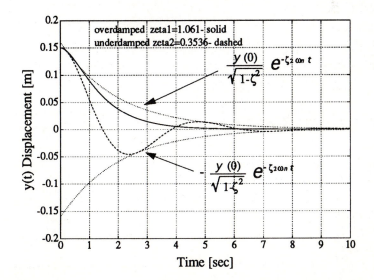

Figure 2.3 Spring-Mass-Damper Unforced Response.

subject to a variety of inputs and initial conditions, it is not feasible to attempt to obtain the solution analytically. In these cases, we can use *MATLAB* to compute the solutions numerically and to display the solution graphically. The simulation capability of *MATLAB* will be discussed in detail in subsequent sections and chapters.

2.3   Transfer Functions

The transfer function is an input-output description of an LTI system, as described in *MCS, pp. 52-63*. It relates the Laplace transform of the output variable to the Laplace transform of the input variable with zero initial conditions. Consider the LTI system described by the transfer function $G(s)$, where

$$G(s) = \frac{Y(s)}{R(s)} = \frac{a_m s^m + a_{m-1} s^{m-1} + \cdots + a_1 s + a_0}{s^n + b_{n-1} s^{n-1} + \cdots + a_1 s + b_0}, \qquad (2.3)$$

where $m \leq n$, and all common factors have been canceled. The roots of the numerator polynomial of $G(s)$ are called the *zeros* of the system; the roots of the denominator polynomial are called the *poles*. Setting the denominator polynomial to zero yields the *characteristic equation*

$$s^n + b_{n-1} s^{n-1} + \cdots + a_1 s + b_0 = 0.$$

The transient response of a system is directly related to the s-plane locations of the poles and zeros.

We can use *MATLAB* to analyze systems described by transfer functions. Since the transfer function is a ratio of polynomials, we begin by investigating how *MATLAB* handles polynomials, remembering that working with transfer functions means that both a numerator polynomial and a denominator polynomial must be specified.

In *MATLAB* polynomials are represented by row vectors containing the polynomial coefficients in descending order. For example, the polynomial

$$p(s) = s^3 + 3s^2 + 4 \qquad (2.4)$$

is entered as shown in Figure 2.4. Notice that even though the

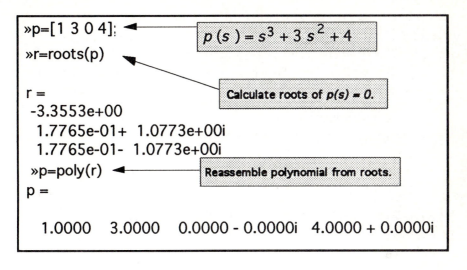

Figure 2.4 Entering the Polynomial $p(s) = s^3 + 3s^2 + 4$ and Calculating Its Roots.

coefficient of the s term is zero, it is included in the input definition of $p(s)$.

If p is a row vector containing the coefficients of $p(s)$ in descending order, then **roots(p)** is a column vector containing the roots of the polynomial. Conversely, if r is a column vector containing the roots of the polynomial, then **poly(r)** is a row vector with the polynomial coefficients in descending order. We can compute the roots of the polynomial $p(s)$, given in Eq. (2.4), with the **roots** function as shown in Figure 2.4. The **roots1** function also computes the roots of a polynomial but gives a more accurate result when the polynomial has repeated roots. In Figure 2.4 we also show how to reassemble the polynomial with the **poly** function.

Multiplication of polynomials is accomplished with the **conv** function. Suppose we want to expand the polynomial $n(s)$, where

$$n(s) = (3s^2 + 2s + 1)(s + 4).$$

The associated *MATLAB* commands using the **conv** function are shown in Figure 2.5. Thus, the expanded polynomial, given by n, is

$$n(s) = 3s^3 + 14s^2 + 9s + 4.$$

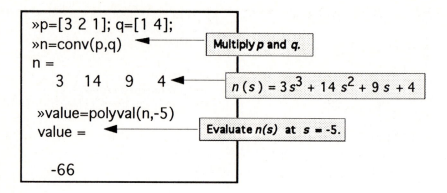

Figure 2.5 Using **conv** and **polyval** to Multiply and Evaluate the Polynomials $(3s^2 + 2s + 1)(s + 4)$.

The function **polyval** is used to evaluate the value of a polynomial at the given value of the variable. The polynomial $n(s)$ has the value $n(-5) = -66$, as shown in Figure 2.5.

In the next example we will obtain a plot of the pole-zero locations in the complex plane. This will be accomplished using the **pzmap** function, shown in Figure 2.6. On the pole-zero map, zeros are denoted by an "o" and poles are denoted by an "x". If the **pzmap** function is invoked without left-hand arguments, the plot is automatically generated.

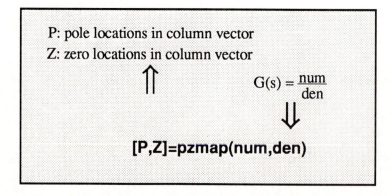

Figure 2.6 The **pzmap** Function.

■ EXAMPLE 2.1 Transfer Functions

Consider the transfer functions

$$G(s) = \frac{6s^2 + 1}{s^3 + 3s^2 + 3s + 1} \quad \text{and} \quad H(s) = \frac{(s+1)(s+2)}{(s+2i)(s-2i)(s+3)}.$$

Utilizing a *MATLAB* script, we can compute the poles and zeros of $G(s)$, the characteristic equation of $H(s)$, and divide $G(s)$ by $H(s)$. We can also obtain a plot of the pole-zero map of $G(s)/H(s)$ in the complex plane.

The pole-zero map of the transfer function $G(s)/H(s)$ is shown in Figure 2.7, and the associated *MATLAB* commands are shown in Figure 2.8. The pole-zero map shows clearly the five zero locations, but it appears that there are only two poles. This cannot be the case since we know that the number of poles must be greater than or equal to the number of zeros. Using the **roots1** function we can ascertain that there are in fact four poles at $s = -1$. Hence, multiple poles or multiple zeros at the same location cannot be discerned on the pole-zero map.

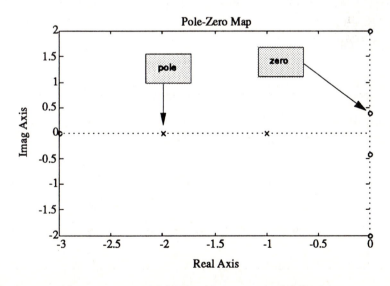

Figure 2.7 Pole-Zero Map for $G(s)/H(s)$.

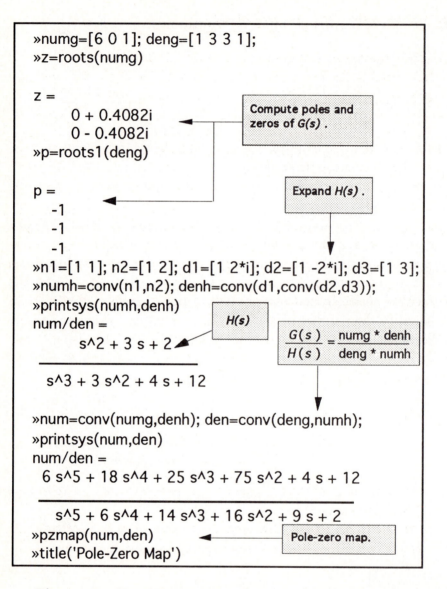

```
»numg=[6 0 1]; deng=[1 3 3 1];
»z=roots(numg)

z =
      0 + 0.4082i                    Compute poles and
      0 - 0.4082i                    zeros of G(s) .
»p=roots1(deng)

p =                                  Expand H(s) .
    -1
    -1
    -1
»n1=[1 1]; n2=[1 2]; d1=[1 2*i]; d2=[1 -2*i]; d3=[1 3];
»numh=conv(n1,n2); denh=conv(d1,conv(d2,d3));
»printsys(numh,denh)
num/den =            H(s)                G(s)     numg * denh
      s^2 + 3 s + 2                      ─────  = ───────────
                                         H(s)     deng * numh
      ──────────────────
      s^3 + 3 s^2 + 4 s + 12

»num=conv(numg,denh); den=conv(deng,numh);
»printsys(num,den)
num/den =
    6 s^5 + 18 s^4 + 25 s^3 + 75 s^2 + 4 s + 12

    ─────────────────────────────────────────────
      s^5 + 6 s^4 + 14 s^3 + 16 s^2 + 9 s + 2
»pzmap(num,den)              ◄───  Pole-zero map.
»title('Pole-Zero Map')
```

Figure 2.8 Transfer Function Example for $G(s)$ and $H(s)$.

2.4 Block Diagram Models

Suppose we have developed mathematical models in the form of transfer functions for the plant, represented by $G(s)$, and the controller, represented by $H(s)$, and possibly many other system components such as sensors and actuators. Our objective is to interconnect these components to form a control system. We will utilize *MATLAB* functions to carry out the block diagram transformations. Block diagram models are described in *MCS, pp. 64-69*.

The process to be controlled is shown in Figure 2.9. A simple open-loop control system can be obtained by interconnecting the plant and the controller in series as illustrated in Figure 2.10. We can use *MATLAB* to compute the transfer function from $R(s)$ to $Y(s)$, as illustrated in Example 2.2.

■ EXAMPLE 2.2 Series Connection

Let the process, represented by the transfer function $G(s)$, be

$$G(s) = \frac{1}{500s^2},$$

and let the controller, represented by the transfer function $G_c(s)$, be

$$G_c(s) = \frac{s+1}{s+2}.$$

We can use the **series** function to cascade two transfer functions $G_1(s)$ and $G_2(s)$, as shown in Figure 2.11.

The transfer function $G_cG(s)$ is computed using the **series** function as shown in Figure 2.12. The resulting transfer function, $G_cG(s)$,

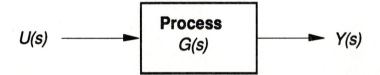

Figure 2.9 Open-Loop System.

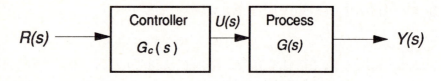

Figure 2.10 Open-Loop Control System.

is

$$G_c G(s) = \frac{\text{num}}{\text{den}} = \frac{s+1}{500s^3 + 1000s^2}.$$

Block diagrams quite often have transfer functions in *parallel*. In such cases, the function **parallel** can be quite useful. The **parallel** function is described in Figure 2.13.

We can introduce a *feedback signal* into the control system by closing the loop with *unity* feedback, as shown in Figure 2.14. The signal $E_a(s)$ is an *error signal*; the signal $R(s)$ is a *reference input*. In this control system, the controller is in the forward path and the closed-loop transfer function is

$$T(s) = \frac{G_c G(s)}{1 \pm G_c G(s)}.$$

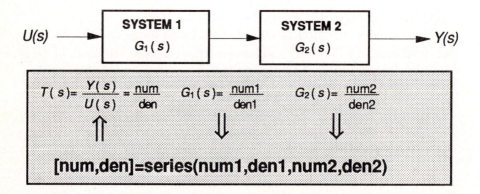

Figure 2.11 The **series** Function.

$$R(s) \longrightarrow \boxed{G_c(s) = \frac{s+1}{s+2}} \xrightarrow{U(s)} \boxed{G(s) = \frac{1}{500\ s^2}} \longrightarrow Y(s)$$

```
»numg=[1]; deng=[500 0 0];
»numh=[1 1]; denh=[1 2];
»[num,den]=series(numg,deng,numh,denh);
»printsys(num,den)
num/den =

           s + 1
  _____
  500 s^3 + 1000 s^2
```

$$\boxed{G_c\ G(s)}$$

Figure 2.12 Application of the **series** Function.

There are two functions we can utilize to aid in the block diagram reduction process to compute closed-loop transfer functions for single- and multi-loop control systems. These functions are **cloop** and **feedback**.

The **cloop** function calculates the closed-loop transfer function

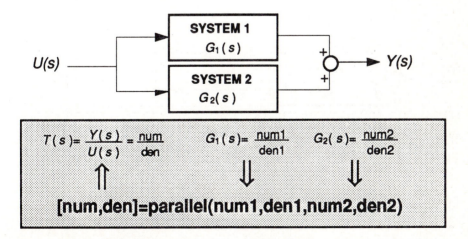

Figure 2.13 The **parallel** Function.

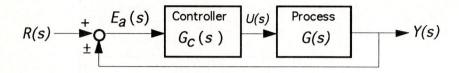

Figure 2.14 A Basic Control System with Unity Feedback.

as shown in Figure 2.15 with the associated system configuration and assumes unity feedback with negative feedback as the default.

The **feedback** function is shown in Figure 2.16 with the associated system configuration, which includes $H(s)$ in the feedback path. For both the **cloop** and **feedback** functions, if the input "sign" is omitted, then negative feedback is assumed. In Example 2.3 we show an application of the **cloop** function, and in Example 2.4 we show an application of the **feedback** function.

■ **EXAMPLE 2.3** The cloop Function

Let the process, $G(s)$, and the controller, $G_c(s)$, be as in Example 2.2 (see Figure 2.12). To apply the **cloop** function we first use the **series** function to compute $G_cG(s)$, followed by the **cloop** function to close the loop. The command sequence is shown in Figure 2.17. The closed-loop transfer function, as shown in Figure 2.17, is

$$T(s) = \frac{G_cG(s)}{1 + G_cG(s)} = \frac{\text{num}}{\text{den}} = \frac{s+1}{500s^3 + 1000s^2 + s + 1}.$$

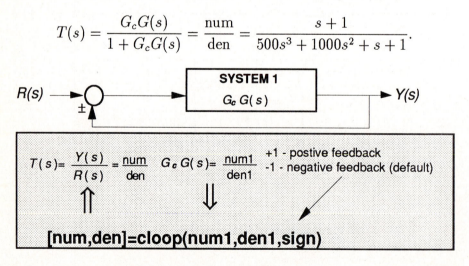

Figure 2.15 The **cloop** Function.

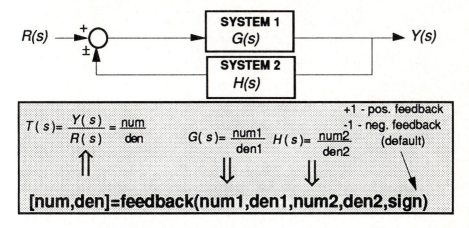

Figure 2.16 The **feedback** Function.

Another basic feedback control configuration is shown in Figure 2.18. In this case, the controller is located in the feedback path. The *error signal*, $E_a(s)$, is also utilized in this control system configuration. The closed-loop transfer function is

$$T(s) = \frac{G(s)}{1 \pm GH(s)}.$$

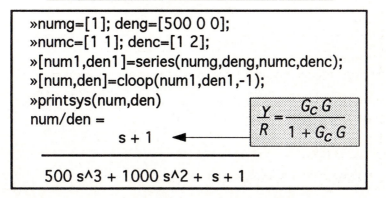

Figure 2.17 Application of the **cloop** Function.

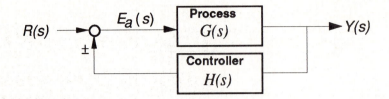

Figure 2.18 A Basic Control System with the Controller in the Feedback Loop.

■ **EXAMPLE 2.4 The feedback Function**

Again, let the process, $G(s)$, and the controller, $H(s)$, be as in Example 2.2 (i.e., $H(s) = G_c(s)$). To compute the closed-loop transfer function with the controller in the feedback loop we use the **feedback** function. The command sequence is shown in Figure 2.19. The closed-loop transfer function is

$$T(s) = \frac{G(s)}{1 + GH(s)} = \frac{\text{num}}{\text{den}} = \frac{s + 2}{500s^3 + 1000s^2 + s + 1}.$$

The *MATLAB* functions **series**, **cloop**, and **feedback** can be used

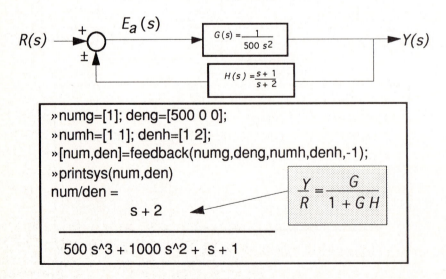

Figure 2.19 Application of the **feedback** Function.

as aids in block diagram manipulations for multi-loop block diagrams. This is illustrated in Example 2.5.

■ EXAMPLE 2.5 Multi-Loop Reduction

A multi-loop feedback system is shown in Figure 2.20. This example can be found in *MCS, pp.67-69*. Our objective is to compute the closed-loop transfer function

$$T(s) = \frac{Y(s)}{R(s)},$$

when

$$G_1(s) = \frac{1}{s+10}, \quad G_2(s) = \frac{1}{s+1},$$

$$G_3(s) = \frac{s^2+1}{s^2+4s+4}, \quad G_4(s) = \frac{s+1}{s+6},$$

and

$$H_1(s) = \frac{s+1}{s+2}, \quad H_2(s) = 2, \quad H_3(s) = 1.$$

For this example, a five-step procedure is followed:

- Step 1: Input the system transfer functions into *MATLAB* .

- Step 2: Move H_2 behind G_4.

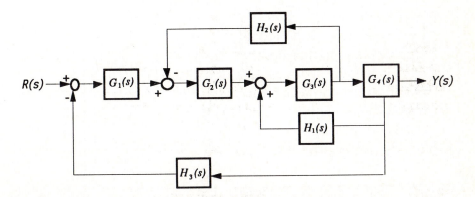

Figure 2.20 Multi-Loop Feedback Control System.

- Step 3: Eliminate the $G_3G_4H_1$ loop.

- Step 4: Eliminate the loop containing H_2.

- Step 5: Eliminate the remaining loop and calculate $T(s)$.

The five steps are illustrated in Figure 2.21, and the corresponding block diagram reduction is shown in Figure 2.22.   The result of executing the *MATLAB* commands is

$$\frac{\text{num}}{\text{den}} = \frac{s^5 + 4s^4 + 6s^3 + 6s^2 + 5s + 2}{12s^6 + 205s^5 + 1066s^4 + 2517s^3 + 3128s^2 + 2196s + 712}.$$

We must be careful in calling this the closed-loop transfer function. Recall that the transfer function is defined to the input-output relationship *after* pole-zero cancellations. If we compute the poles and zeros of $T(s)$, we find that the numerator and denominator polynomials have $(s + 1)$ as a common factor. This must be canceled before we can claim we have the closed-loop transfer function. To

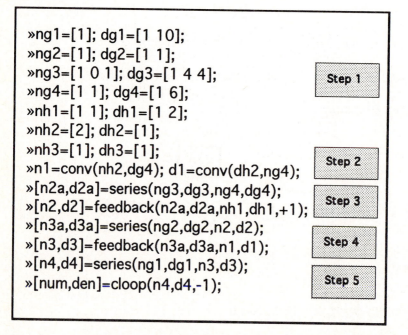

```
»ng1=[1]; dg1=[1 10];
»ng2=[1]; dg2=[1 1];
»ng3=[1 0 1]; dg3=[1 4 4];          Step 1
»ng4=[1 1]; dg4=[1 6];
»nh1=[1 1]; dh1=[1 2];
»nh2=[2]; dh2=[1];
»nh3=[1]; dh3=[1];
»n1=conv(nh2,dg4); d1=conv(dh2,ng4);   Step 2
»[n2a,d2a]=series(ng3,dg3,ng4,dg4);
»[n2,d2]=feedback(n2a,d2a,nh1,dh1,+1);   Step 3
»[n3a,d3a]=series(ng2,dg2,n2,d2);
»[n3,d3]=feedback(n3a,d3a,n1,d1);     Step 4
»[n4,d4]=series(ng1,dg1,n3,d3);
»[num,den]=cloop(n4,d4,-1);        Step 5
```

Figure 2.21 Multi-Loop Block Reduction.

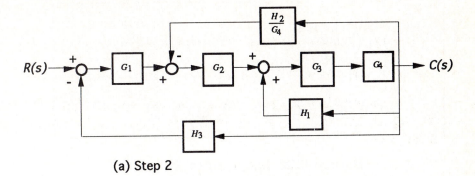

(a) Step 2

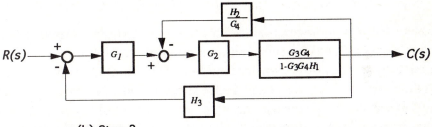

(b) Step 3

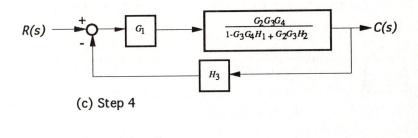

(c) Step 4

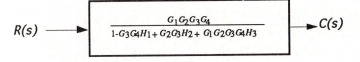

(d) Step 5

Figure 2.22 Block Diagram Reduction of Multi-Loop System (See Example 2.5 in *MCS, pp. 67-69*).

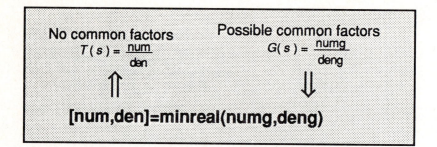

Figure 2.23 The **minreal** Function.

assist us in the pole-zero cancellation we will use the **minreal** function. The **minreal** function, shown in Figure 2.23, removes common
pole-zero factors of a transfer function. The final step in the block
reduction process is to cancel out the common factors, as shown
in Figure 2.24. The closed-loop transfer function is given in Figure 2.24 as $T(s) = $ num/den. After the application of the **minreal**
function we find that the order of the denominator polynomial has
been reduced from six to five, implying one pole-zero cancellation.

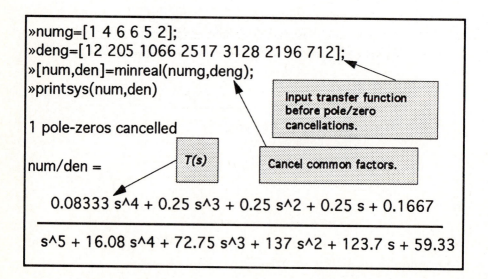

Figure 2.24 Application of the **minreal** Function.

2.5 Design Example

Electric traction motors are utilized on trains and transit vehicles. The detailed block diagram model with the transfer functions of the power amplifier, armature controlled motor, and sensor, is shown in Figure 2.25. This is Example 2.9 in *MCS, pp. 79-81*. Our objective is to compute the closed-loop transfer function and investigate the response of ω to a commanded ω_d. The first step, as shown in Figure 2.26, is to compute the closed-loop transfer function ω/ω_d. The closed-loop characteristic equation is second-order with $\omega_n = 52$ and $\zeta = 0.012$. Since the damping is low we might expect the response to be highly oscillatory. We can investigate the response $\omega(t)$ to a reference input, $\omega_d(t)$, by utilizing the **step** function. The **step** function, shown in Figure 2.27, calculates the unit step response of a linear system.

The **step** function is a very important function since control system performance specifications are often given in terms of the unit step response. The state response, given by $x(t)$, is an output of the **step** function and will be discussed in detail in Chapter 9, State-Space Methods. Include x in the left-hand argument list, but do not be concerned with it for the time being.

If the only objective is to plot the output, $y(t)$, we can use the **step** function without left-hand arguments and obtain the plot automatically with axis labels. If we need $y(t)$ for any reason other than plotting, we must use the **step** function with left-hand arguments, followed by the **plot** function to plot $y(t)$. We define t as a

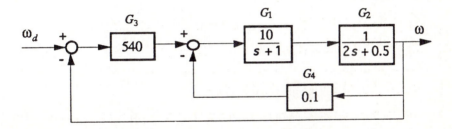

Figure 2.25 Electric Traction Motor Block Diagram.

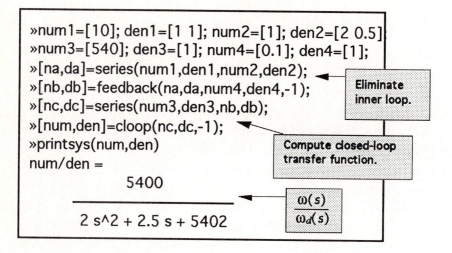

Figure 2.26 Electric Traction Motor Block Reduction.

row vector containing the times at which we wish the value of the output variable $y(t)$.

The step response of the electric traction motor is shown in Figure 2.28. As expected, the wheel velocity response, given by $y(t)$, is highly oscillatory.

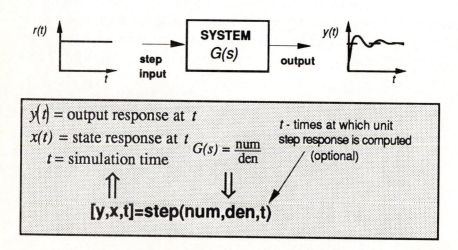

Figure 2.27 The **step** Function.

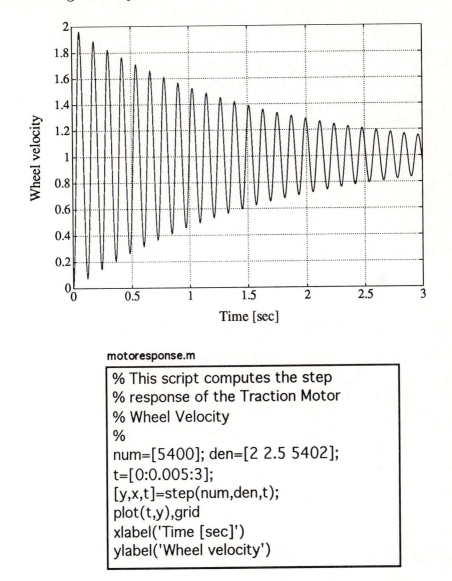

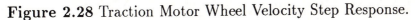

motoresponse.m

```
% This script computes the step
% response of the Traction Motor
% Wheel Velocity
%
num=[5400]; den=[2 2.5 5402];
t=[0:0.005:3];
[y,x,t]=step(num,den,t);
plot(t,y),grid
xlabel('Time [sec]')
ylabel('Wheel velocity')
```

Figure 2.28 Traction Motor Wheel Velocity Step Response.

_____ Notes _____

Chapter 3

Control System Characteristics

3.1 Introduction

We introduce *feedback* to

1. decrease the sensitivity of the system to plant variations,

2. enable adjustment of the system transient response,

3. reject disturbances, and

4. reduce steady-state tracking errors.

The advantages of feedback (listed above) come at the cost of increasing the number of components and system complexity, reduction in the closed-loop system gain, and the introduction of possible instabilities. However, the advantages of feedback outweigh the disadvantages to such an extent that feedback control systems are found everywhere. In this chapter, the advantages of feedback are illustrated with two examples. Our objective is to illustrate the use of *MATLAB* in the control system analysis.

In the first example, we introduce feedback control to a speed tachometer system in an effort to reject disturbances. The tachometer speed control system example can be found in *MCS, pp. 125-128*.

The reduction in system sensitivity to plant variations, adjustment of the transient response, and reduction in steady-state error are demonstrated in a second example. This is the English Channel boring machine example found in *MCS, pp. 134-137*.

49

3.2   Speed Tachometer System

The open-loop block diagram description of the armature controlled dc-motor with a load torque disturbance, $T_d(s)$, is shown in Figure 3.1. The values for the various parameters, taken from Example 2.9 in *MCS, pp. 79-81*, are given in Table 3.1. We have two inputs to our system, $V_a(s)$ and $T_d(s)$. Relying on the *principal of superposition*, which applies to our LTI system, we consider each input separately. To investigate the effects of disturbances on the system, we let $V_a(s) = 0$ and consider only the disturbance $T_d(s)$. Conversely, to investigate the response of the system to a reference input, we let $T_d(s) = 0$ and consider only the input $V_a(s)$.

The closed-loop speed tachometer control system block diagram is shown in Figure 3.2. The values for K_a and K_t are given in Table 3.1.

If our system displays good disturbance rejection, then we expect the disturbance $T_d(s)$ to have a small effect on the output $\omega(s)$. Consider the open-loop system shown in Figure 3.1 first. We can use *MATLAB* to compute the transfer function from $T_d(s)$ to $\omega(s)$ and evaluate the output response to a unit step disturbance (i.e., $T_d(s) = 1/s$). The time response to a unit step disturbance is shown in Figure 3.3. The *script* **opentach.m**, shown in Figure 3.3, is used to analyze the open-loop speed tachometer system.

The open-loop transfer function is

$$\frac{\omega(s)}{T_d(s)} = \frac{\text{num}}{\text{den}} = \frac{-1}{2s + 1.5}.$$

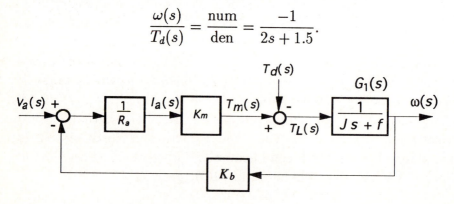

Figure 3.1 Open-Loop Speed Tachometer Control System where K_b is the Back Electromotive-Force Constant.

Table 3.1 Tachometer Control System Parameters.

R_a	K_m	J	f	K_b	K_a	K_t
1	10	2	0.5	0.1	54	1

Since our desired value of $w(t)$ is zero (remember that $V_a(s) = 0$), the steady-state error is just the final value of $w(t)$, which we denote by $w_o(t)$ to indicate open-loop. The steady-state error, shown on the plot in Figure 3.3, is approximately the value of the speed when $t = 7$ seconds. We can obtain an approximate value of the steady-state error by looking at the last value in the output vector y_o, which we generated in the process of making the plot in Figure 3.3. The approximate steady-state value of w_o is

$$w_o(\infty) \approx w_o(7) = -0.6632 \text{ rad/sec}.$$

The plot verifies that we have in fact reached steady-state.

In a similar fashion, we begin the closed-loop system analysis by computing the closed-loop transfer function from $T_d(s)$ to $w(s)$, and then generating the time-response of $w(t)$ to a unit step disturbance input. The output response and the *script* **closedtach.m** are shown in Figure 3.4. The closed-loop transfer function from the disturbance

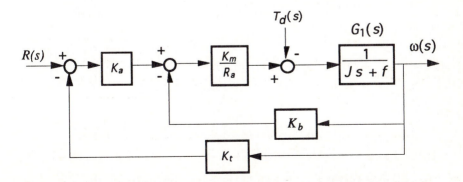

Figure 3.2 Closed-Loop Speed Tachometer Control System.

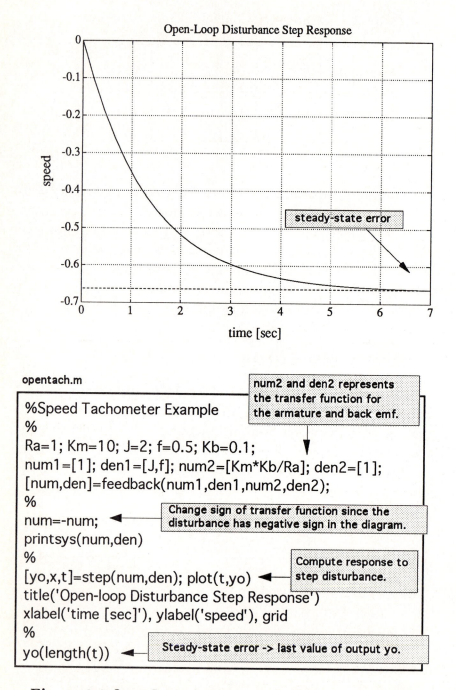

Figure 3.3 Open-Loop Analysis of the Tachometer System.

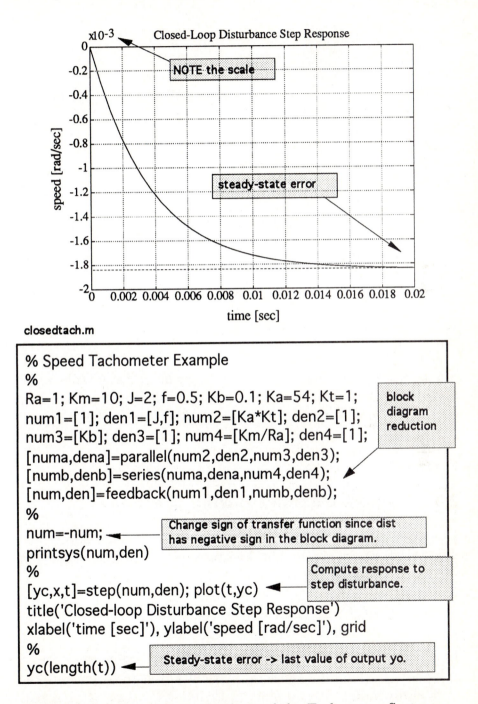

closedtach.m

```
% Speed Tachometer Example
%
Ra=1; Km=10; J=2; f=0.5; Kb=0.1; Ka=54; Kt=1;
num1=[1]; den1=[J,f]; num2=[Ka*Kt]; den2=[1];
num3=[Kb]; den3=[1]; num4=[Km/Ra]; den4=[1];
[numa,dena]=parallel(num2,den2,num3,den3);
[numb,denb]=series(numa,dena,num4,den4);
[num,den]=feedback(num1,den1,numb,denb);
%
num=-num;
printsys(num,den)
%
[yc,x,t]=step(num,den); plot(t,yc)
title('Closed-loop Disturbance Step Response')
xlabel('time [sec]'), ylabel('speed [rad/sec]'), grid
%
yc(length(t))
```

block diagram reduction

Change sign of transfer function since dist has negative sign in the block diagram.

Compute response to step disturbance.

Steady-state error -> last value of output yo.

Figure 3.4 Closed-Loop Analysis of the Tachometer System.

input is

$$\frac{\omega(s)}{T_d(s)} = \frac{\text{num}}{\text{den}} = \frac{-1}{2s + 541.5}.$$

As before, the steady-state error is just the final value of $\omega(t)$, which we denote by $\omega_c(t)$ to indicate closed-loop. The steady-state error is shown on the plot in Figure 3.4. We can obtain an approximate value of the steady-state error by looking at the last value in the output vector y_c, which we generated in the process of making the plot in Figure 3.4. The approximate steady-state value of ω is

$$\omega_c(\infty) \approx \omega_c(0.02) = -0.0018 \quad \text{rad/sec}.$$

We generally expect that $\omega_c(\infty)/\omega_o(\infty) < 0.02$. The ratio of closed-loop to open-loop steady-state speed output due to a unit step disturbance input, in this example, is

$$\frac{\omega_c(\infty)}{\omega_o(\infty)} = 0.0027.$$

We have achieved a remarkable improvement in disturbance rejection. It is clear that the addition of the negative feedback loop reduced the effect of the disturbance on the output. This demonstrates the *disturbance rejection* property of closed-loop feedback systems.

3.3   English Channel Boring Machines

The block diagram description of the English Channel boring machines is shown in Figure 3.5. The transfer function of the output due to the two inputs is

$$C(s) = \frac{K}{s^2 + 12s + K}R(s) + \frac{1}{s^2 + 12s + K}D(s).$$

The effect of the control gain K on the transient response is shown in Figure 3.6 along with the *script* **english1.m** used to generate the plots. Comparing the two plots in Figure 3.6, it can be seen that decreasing K decreases the *overshoot*. Although it is not as obvious

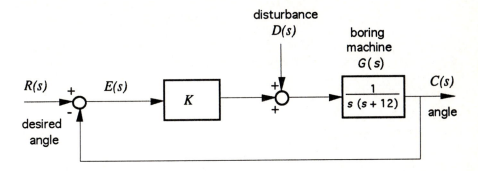

Figure 3.5 Boring Machine Control System Block Diagram.

from the plots in Figure 3.6, it is also true that decreasing K decreases the *settling time*. This can be verified by taking a closer look (at the command level) at the data used to generate the plots. This example demonstrates how the transient response can be altered by feedback control gain K. Based on our analysis thus far, we would prefer to use $K = 50$. However, there are other considerations that must be taken into account before we can establish the final design.

Before making the final choice of K, it is important to consider the system response to a unit step disturbance. This is shown in Figure 3.7. We see that increasing K reduces the steady-state response of $c(t)$ to the step disturbance. The steady-state value of $c(t)$ is 0.02 and 0.01 for $K = 50$ and 100, respectively. The steady-state errors, percent overshoot, and settling times are summarized in Table 3.2. The steady-state values are predicted from the *final value theorem* as follows:

$$\lim_{t \to \infty} c(t) = \lim_{s \to 0} s \cdot \frac{1}{s(s + 12) + K} \cdot \frac{1}{s} = \frac{1}{K}.$$

If our only design consideration is disturbance rejection, we would prefer to use $K = 100$.

We have just experienced a very common *trade-off* situation in control system design. In this particular example, increasing K leads to better disturbance rejection, while decreasing K leads to better performance (via less overshoot and quicker settling time). The final

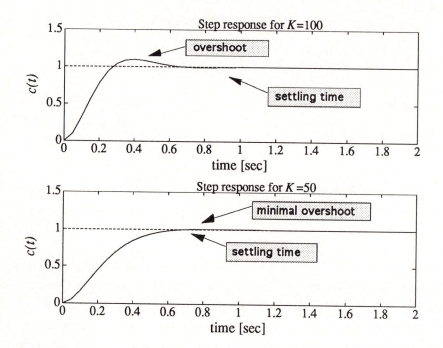

english1.m

```
% Response to a Unit Step Input R(s)=1/s for K=50, 100
%
numg=[1]; deng=[1 12 0]; K1=100; K2=50;
num1=K1*numg; num2=K2*numg;
%                    closed-loop transfer functions
[numa,dena]=cloop(num1,deng);
[numb,denb]=cloop(num2,deng);
%                                    Create subplots with
                       Choose time interval.    x and y axis labels.
t=[0:0.05:2.0];
[y1,x,t]=step(numa,dena,t); [y2,x,t]=step(numb,denb,t);
subplot(211),plot(t,y1), title('Step Response for K=100')
xlabel('time [sec]'),ylabel('c(t)')
subplot(212),plot(t,y2), title('Step Response for K=50')
xlabel('time [sec]'),ylabel('c(t)')
```

Figure 3.6 The Response to a Step Input with $K=100$ and $K=50$.

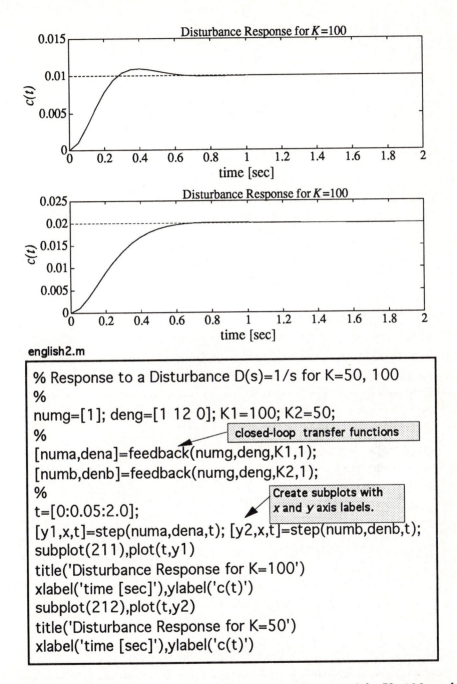

Figure 3.7 The Response to a Step Disturbance with $K=100$ and $K=50$.

Table 3.2 Response of the Boring Machine Control System for $K = 50$ and $K = 100$.

	$K = 50$	$K = 100$
P.O.	0	10
T_s	1.1	1.3
e_{ss}	2%	1%

decision on how to choose K rests with the designer. So you see that while *MATLAB* can certainly assist you in the control system design, it cannot replace your decision-making capability and intuition.

The final step in the analysis is to look at the system sensitivity to changes in the plant. The system sensitivity is given by (Eq. **3.62**, *MCS, p. 137*)

$$S(s) = \frac{1}{1 + KG(s)}$$

$$= \frac{s(s + 12)}{s(s + 12) + K}.$$

We can compute the values of $S(s)$ for different values of s and generate a plot of the system sensitivity. For low frequencies, we can approximate the system sensitivity by

$$S(s) \approx \frac{12s}{K}.$$

Increasing the gain K reduces the system sensitivity. The system sensitivity plots are shown in Figure **3.8** for $K = 50$. The sensitivity approximation is also shown in Figure **3.8**.

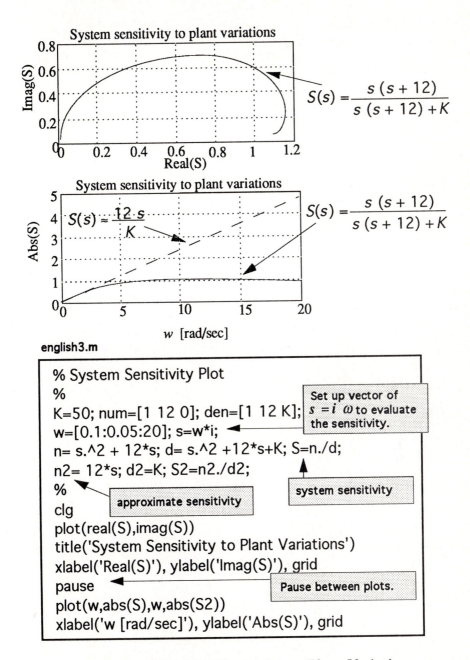

Figure 3.8 System Sensitivity to Plant Variations.

————————————————— Notes —————————————————

Chapter 4

Control System Performance

4.1   Introduction

Primary concerns in control system design are stability and performance. Performance is an issue for stable systems and is the topic of this chapter. In order to design and analyze control systems, we must first establish adequate performance specifications. Performance specifications can be presented in the *time domain* or the *frequency domain*. Time-domain specifications generally take the form of settling time, percent overshoot, rise time, and steady-state error specifications. Stability and frequency-domain specifications are addressed in the next chapters.

This chapter is organized as follows. In the next section we investigate time-domain performance specifications given in terms of transient response to a given input signal and the resulting *steady-state tracking errors*. The chapter concludes with a discussion of simplification of linear systems.

The *MATLAB* functions introduced in this chapter are **impulse** and **lsim**. These functions are used to simulate linear systems.

4.2   Time-Domain Specifications

Time-domain performance specifications are generally given in terms of the transient response of a system to a given input signal. Since the actual input signals are generally unknown, a standard *test input*

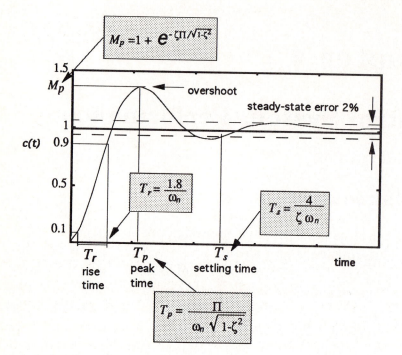

Figure 4.1 Step Response of a Second-Order System.

signal is used. The test signals are of the general form

$$r(t) = t^n,$$

and the corresponding Laplace transform is

$$R(s) = \frac{n!}{s^{n+1}}.$$

When $n = 1, 2$, and 3 we have the step, ramp, and parabolic inputs, respectively. An *impulse* function is also used as a test signal.

The *standard* performance measures are usually defined in terms of the step response and the impulse response. The most common step response performance measures are percent overshoot (P.O.), rise time (T_r), peak time (T_p), and settling time (T_s), as shown in Figure 4.1.

Consider the second-order system shown in Figure 4.2. The

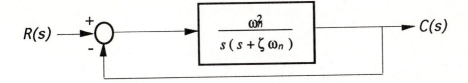

Figure 4.2 Single-Loop Second-Order Feedback System.

closed-loop output is

$$C(s) = \frac{\omega_n^2}{s^2 + 2\zeta\omega_n s + \omega_n^2} \, R(s).$$

We have already discussed the use of the **step** function to compute the step response of a system. Now we address another important test signal: the impulse. The impulse response is the time derivative of the step response. We compute the impulse response with the **impulse** function shown in Figure 4.3.

We can obtain a plot similar to Figure 4.5(a) in *MCS, p. 162* with the **step** function, as shown in Figure 4.4. Using the **impulse** function, we can obtain a plot similar to Figure 4.6 in *MCS, p. 163*. The response of a second-order system for an impulse function input is shown in Figure 4.5. In the script, we set $\omega_n = 1$, which is

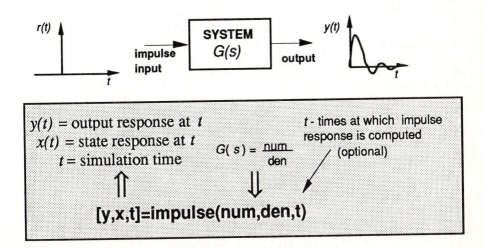

Figure 4.3 The **impulse** Function.

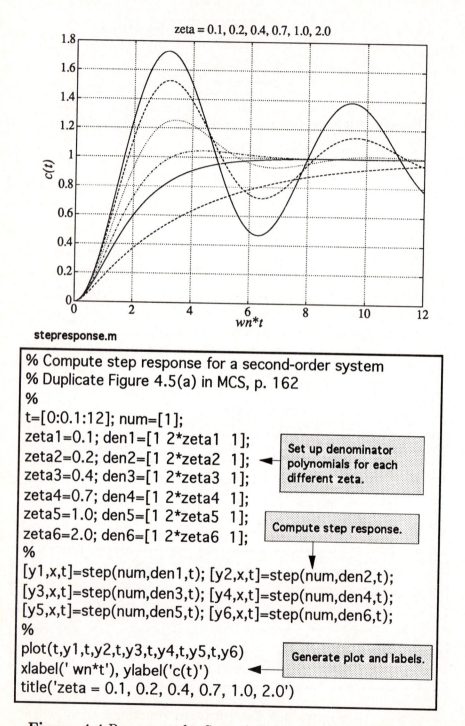

stepresponse.m

```
% Compute step response for a second-order system
% Duplicate Figure 4.5(a) in MCS, p. 162
%
t=[0:0.1:12]; num=[1];
zeta1=0.1; den1=[1 2*zeta1 1];        ┌─────────────────────┐
zeta2=0.2; den2=[1 2*zeta2 1];   ◄────│ Set up denominator  │
zeta3=0.4; den3=[1 2*zeta3 1];        │ polynomials for each│
zeta4=0.7; den4=[1 2*zeta4 1];        │ different zeta.     │
zeta5=1.0; den5=[1 2*zeta5 1];        └─────────────────────┘
zeta6=2.0; den6=[1 2*zeta6 1];        ┌─────────────────────┐
%                                     │ Compute step response.│
[y1,x,t]=step(num,den1,t); [y2,x,t]=step(num,den2,t);
[y3,x,t]=step(num,den3,t); [y4,x,t]=step(num,den4,t);
[y5,x,t]=step(num,den5,t); [y6,x,t]=step(num,den6,t);
%
plot(t,y1,t,y2,t,y3,t,y4,t,y5,t,y6)  ┌─────────────────────┐
xlabel(' wn*t'), ylabel('c(t)')  ◄───│ Generate plot and labels.│
title('zeta = 0.1, 0.2, 0.4, 0.7, 1.0, 2.0')
```

Figure 4.4 Response of a Second-Order System to a Step.

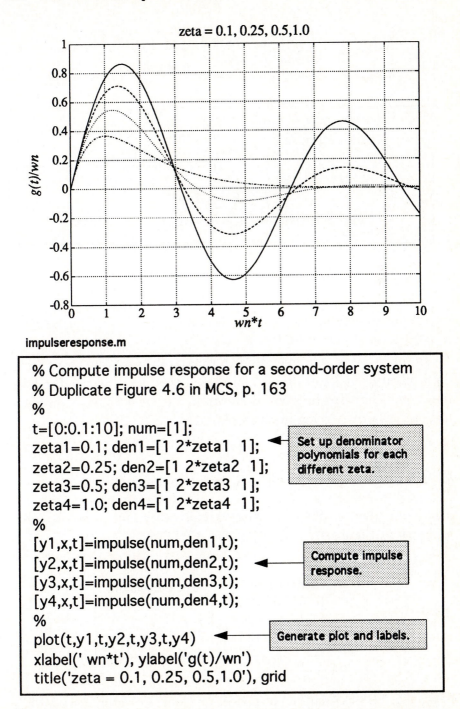

impulseresponse.m

```
% Compute impulse response for a second-order system
% Duplicate Figure 4.6 in MCS, p. 163
%
t=[0:0.1:10]; num=[1];
zeta1=0.1; den1=[1 2*zeta1  1];          Set up denominator
zeta2=0.25; den2=[1 2*zeta2  1];         polynomials for each
zeta3=0.5; den3=[1 2*zeta3  1];          different zeta.
zeta4=1.0; den4=[1 2*zeta4  1];
%
[y1,x,t]=impulse(num,den1,t);
[y2,x,t]=impulse(num,den2,t);            Compute impulse
[y3,x,t]=impulse(num,den3,t);            response.
[y4,x,t]=impulse(num,den4,t);
%
plot(t,y1,t,y2,t,y3,t,y4)                Generate plot and labels.
xlabel(' wn*t'), ylabel('g(t)/wn')
title('zeta = 0.1, 0.25, 0.5,1.0'), grid
```

Figure 4.5 Response of a Second-Order System to an Impulse.

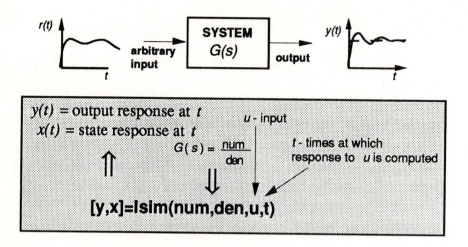

Figure 4.6 The lsim Function.

equivalent to computing the step response versus $\omega_n t$. This gives us a more general plot valid for any $\omega_n > 0$.

In many cases, you may need to simulate the system response to an arbitrary but known input. In these cases, you can use the **lsim** function. The **lsim** function is shown in Figure 4.6. An example of the use of **lsim** is given in Example 4.1.

■ EXAMPLE 4.1 Mobile Robot Steering Control

The block diagram for a steering control system for a mobile robot is shown in Figure 4.7 (see *MCS, pp. 174-176*).

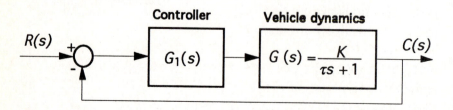

Figure 4.7 Block Diagram of a Steering Control System for a Mobile Robot.

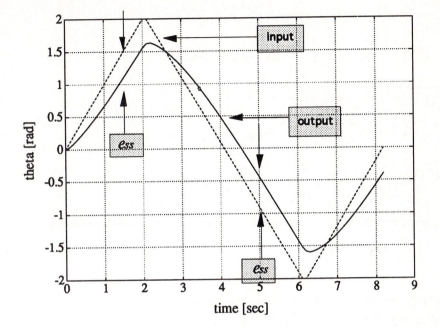

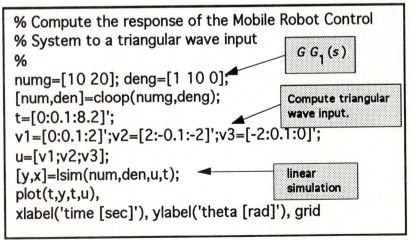

mobilerobot.m

```
% Compute the response of the Mobile Robot Control
% System to a triangular wave input
%
numg=[10 20]; deng=[1 10 0];
[num,den]=cloop(numg,deng);
t=[0:0.1:8.2]';
v1=[0:0.1:2]';v2=[2:-0.1:-2]';v3=[-2:0.1:0]';
u=[v1;v2;v3];
[y,x]=lsim(num,den,u,t);
plot(t,y,t,u),
xlabel('time [sec]'), ylabel('theta [rad]'), grid
```

Figure 4.8 Transient Response of the Mobile Robot Steering Control System to a Ramp Input.

Suppose the steering controller, $G_1(s)$, is

$$G_1(s) = K_1 + \frac{K_s}{s}.$$

When the input is a ramp, the steady-state error is

$$e_{ss} = \frac{A}{K_v}, \tag{4.1}$$

where

$$K_v = K_2 K.$$

The effect of the controller constant, K_2, on the steady-state error is evident from Eq. (4.1). Whenever K_2 is large, the steady-state error is small, and vice versa.

We can simulate the closed-loop system response to a ramp input using the **lsim** function. The controller gains K_1, K_2 and the system gain K can be represented symbolically in the script so that various values can be selected and simulated. The results are shown in Figure 4.8 for $K_1 = K = 1$, $K_2 = 2$, and $\tau = 1/10$.

4.3   Simplification of Linear Systems

In practice, it may be necessary to approximate a higher-order transfer function model with a lower-order model. For example, it may be impractical to implement a high-order controller in a control system. However, it may be possible to develop a lower-order approximate controller that closely matches the input-output response of the high-order controller. A procedure for approximating transfer functions is given in *MCS, pp. 185-187*. We can use *MATLAB* to compare the approximate model to the actual model, as illustrated in the following example.

■ **EXAMPLE 4.2 A Simplified Model**

Consider the third-order system

$$H(s) = \frac{6}{s^3 + 6s^2 + 11s + 6}.$$

A second-order approximation (see *MCS, pp. 187-188*) is

$$L(s) = \frac{1.60}{s^2 + 2.584s + 1.60}.$$

A comparison of their respective step responses is given in Figure 4.9.

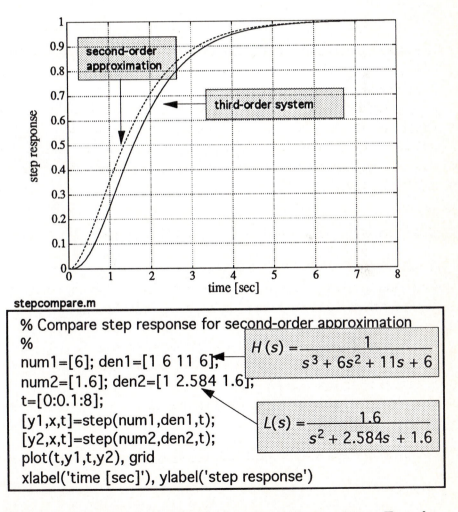

Figure 4.9 Step Response Comparison for an Approximate Transfer Function Versus the Actual Transfer Function.

_____ Notes _____

Chapter 5

Control System Stability

5.1   Introduction

The stability of a closed-loop control system is a fundamental issue in controls. Generally speaking, an unstable closed-loop control system is of little practical value. For linear systems, a necessary and sufficient condition for a feedback system to be stable is that all the poles of the system transfer function have negative real parts. In other words, the poles must lie in the left-half plane for the system to be stable. The Routh-Hurwitz stability method provides a structured mechanism for determining the number of unstable poles of the closed-loop characteristic equation. This allows us to obtain a "yes" or "no" answer to stability without explicitly calculating the poles.

This chapter begins with a discussion of the Routh-Hurwitz stability method. We will see how *MATLAB* can assist us in the stability analysis by providing an easy and accurate method for computing the poles of the characteristic equation. For the case where the characteristic equation is a function of a single parameter, it will be possible to generate a plot displaying the *movement* of the poles as the parameter varies. The chapter concludes with an example.

The function introduced in this chapter is the function **for**, which is used to repeat a number of statements a specific number of times.

5.2 Routh-Hurwitz Stability

The Routh-Hurwitz criterion is a necessary and sufficient criterion
for stability. Given a characteristic equation with fixed coefficients,
we can use Routh-Hurwitz to determine the number of roots in the
right-half plane. For example, consider the characteristic equation

$$q(s) = s^3 + s^2 + 2s + 24 = 0$$

associated with the closed-loop control system shown in Figure 5.1.
The corresponding Routh-Hurwitz array is shown in Figure 5.2. The
two sign changes in the first column indicate that there are two
roots of the characteristic polynomial in the right-half plane; hence
the closed-loop system is unstable. Using *MATLAB* we can verify
the Routh-Hurwitz result by directly computing the roots of the
characteristic equation, as shown in Figure 5.3, using the **roots**
function. Recall that the **roots** function computes the roots of a
polynomial.

Whenever the characteristic equation is a function of a single
parameter, the Routh-Hurwitz method can be utilized to determine
the range of values that the parameter may take while maintaining
stability. Consider the closed-loop feedback system in Figure 5.4.
The characteristic equation is

$$q(s) = s^3 + s^2 + 4s + K = 0.$$

Using a Routh-Hurwitz approach we find that we require $0 \leq K \leq 8$
for stability (see *MCS, p. 215*). We can use *MATLAB* to verify this

Figure 5.1 Closed-Loop Control System with $T(s) = C(s)/R(s) = 1/(s^3 + s^2 + 2s + 24)$.

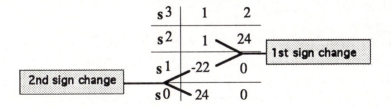

Figure 5.2 Routh-Hurwitz Array for the Closed-Loop Control System with $T(s) = C(s)/R(s) = 1/(s^3 + s^2 + 2s + 24)$.

result graphically. As shown in Figure 5.5, we establish a vector of values for K at which we wish to compute the roots of the characteristic equation. Then using the **roots** function we calculate and plot the roots of the characteristic equation, as shown in Figure 5.5. It can be seen that as K increases, the roots of the characteristic equation move toward the right-half plane as the gain tends toward $K = 8$, and eventually into the right-half plane when $K > 8$. This is a graphical verification of the Routh-Hurwitz result obtained above. In the next chapter we will discover a compact method of obtaining the plot of the root locations as a function of one parameter using the *root locus method*.

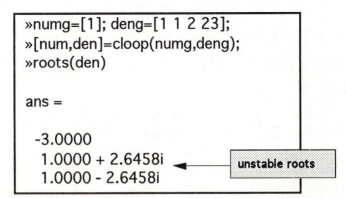

Figure 5.3 Using the **roots** Function to Compute the Closed-Loop Control System Poles of the System Shown in Figure 5.1.

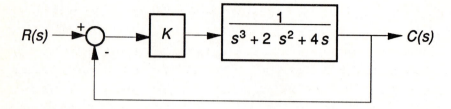

Figure 5.4 Closed-Loop Control System with $T(s) = C(s)/R(s) = K/(s^3 + 2s^2 + 4s + K)$.

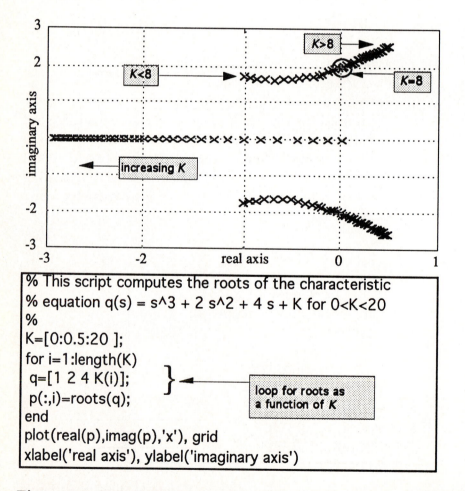

```
% This script computes the roots of the characteristic
% equation q(s) = s^3 + 2 s^2 + 4 s + K for 0<K<20
%
K=[0:0.5:20 ];
for i=1:length(K)
 q=[1 2 4 K(i)];        }◄──── loop for roots as
 p(:,i)=roots(q);                a function of K
end
plot(real(p),imag(p),'x'), grid
xlabel('real axis'), ylabel('imaginary axis')
```

Figure 5.5 Plot of Root Locations of $q(s) = s^3 + 2s^2 + 4s + K$ for $0 \le K \le 20$.

The script in Figure 5.5 contains the **for** function. The **for** function provides a mechanism for repeatedly executing a series of statements a given number of times. The **for** function connected to an **end** statement sets up a repeating calculation loop. Figure 5.6 describes the **for** function format and provides an illustrative example of its usefulness. The example sets up a loop that repeats ten times. During the ith iteration, where $1 \leq i \leq 10$, the ith element of the vector a is set equal to 20 and the scalar b is recomputed.

The Routh-Hurwitz method allows us to make definitive statements regarding absolute stability of a linear system. The method does not address the issue of *relative stability*, which is directly related to the location of the roots of the characteristic equation. Routh-Hurwitz tells us how many poles lie in the right-half plane, but not the specific location of the poles. With *MATLAB* we can easily calculate the poles explicitly, thus allowing us to comment on the system relative stability. We conclude this chapter with an example taken from *MCS, pp. 223-225.*

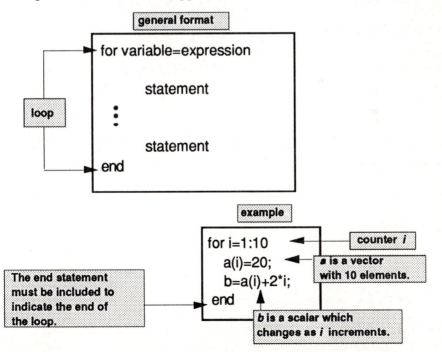

Figure 5.6 The **for** Function and an Illustrative Example.

5.3   Example: Tracked Vehicle Turning Control

The block diagram of the control system for the two-track vehicle
is shown in Figure 5.7. The design objective is to find a and K
such that the system is stable and the steady-state error for a ramp
input is less than or equal to 24% of the command. We can use the
Routh-Hurwitz method to aid in the search for appropriate values
of a and K. The closed-loop characteristic equation is

$$q(s) = s^4 + 8s^3 + 17s^2 + (K+10)s + aK = 0.$$

Using the Routh-Hurwitz array we find that for stability we require

$$K < 126 , \quad aK > 0.$$

For positive K it follows that we can restrict our search to $0 < K <$
126 and $a > 0$. Our approach will be to use *MATLAB* to find a
parameterized a versus K region in which stability is assured. Then
we can find a set of (a, K) belonging to the stable region such that
the steady-state error specification is met. This procedure, shown
in Figure 5.8, involves selecting a range of values for a and K and
computing the roots of the characteristic for specific values of a and
K. For each value of K, we find the first value of a that results in at
least one root of the characteristic equation in the right-half plane.
The process is repeated until the entire selected range of a and K is
exhausted. Then, the plot of the (a, K) pairs defines the separation
between the stable and unstable regions.

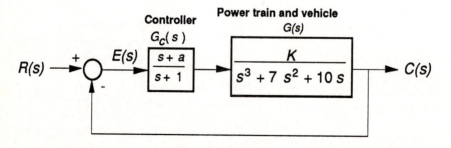

Figure 5.7 Turning Control for a Two-Track Vehicle.

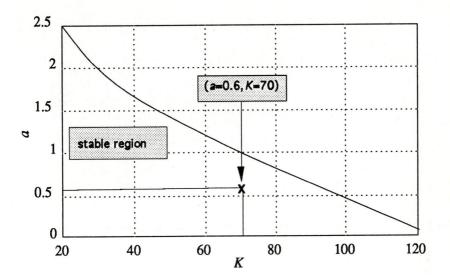

twotrackstable.m

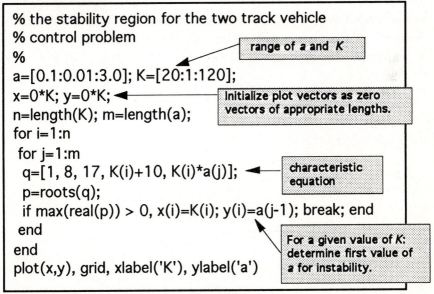

```
% the stability region for the two track vehicle
% control problem
%                              range of a and K
a=[0.1:0.01:3.0]; K=[20:1:120];
x=0*K; y=0*K;          Initialize plot vectors as zero
n=length(K); m=length(a);   vectors of appropriate lengths.
for i=1:n
  for j=1:m
    q=[1, 8, 17, K(i)+10, K(i)*a(j)];   characteristic
    p=roots(q);                          equation
    if max(real(p)) > 0, x(i)=K(i); y(i)=a(j-1); break; end
  end
end                                  For a given value of K:
                                     determine first value of
plot(x,y), grid, xlabel('K'), ylabel('a')   a for instability.
```

Figure 5.8 Stability Region for a and K for Two-Track Vehicle Turning Control.

The region to the left of the plot of a versus K in Figure 5.8 is the stable region, since that corresponds to $K < 126$.

If we assume that $r(t) = At, t > 0$, then the steady-state error is

$$e_{ss} = \lim_{s \to 0} s \cdot \frac{s(s+1)(s+2)(s+5)}{s(s+1)(s+2)(s+5) + K(s+a)} \cdot \frac{A}{s^2} = \frac{10A}{aK},$$

where we have used the fact that

$$E(s) = \frac{1}{1 + G_c G(s)} R(s) = \frac{s(s+1)(s+2)(s+5)}{s(s+1)(s+2)(s+5) + K(s+a)} R(s).$$

Given the steady-state specification, $e_{ss} < 0.24A$, we find that the specification is satisfied when

$$\frac{10A}{aK} < 0.24A,$$

or

$$aK > 41.67. \tag{5.1}$$

Any values of a and K that lie in the stable region in Figure 5.8 and satisfy Eq. (5.1) will lead to an acceptable design. For example, $K = 70$ and $a = 0.6$ will satisfy all the design requirements. The closed-loop transfer function (with $a = 0.6$ and $K = 70$) is

$$T(s) = \frac{70s + 42}{s^4 + 8s^3 + 17s^2 + 80s + 42}.$$

The associated closed-loop poles are

$$
\begin{aligned}
s &= -7.0767, \\
s &= -0.5781, \\
s &= -0.1726 + 3.1995i, \text{ and} \\
s &= -0.1726 - 3.1995i.
\end{aligned}
$$

The corresponding unit ramp input response is shown in Figure 5.9. The steady-state error is less than 0.25, as desired.

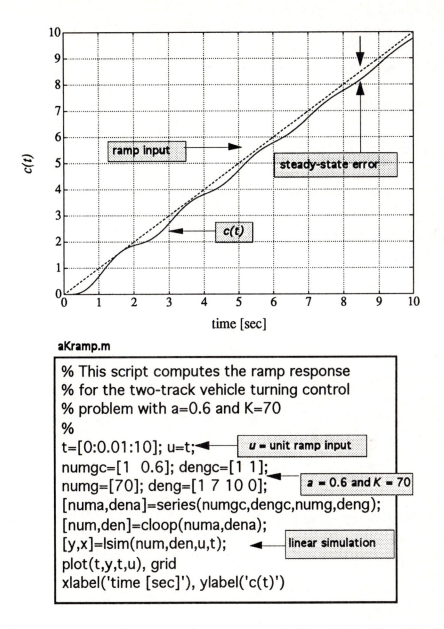

Figure 5.9 Ramp Response for $a = 0.6$ and $K = 70$ for Two-Track Vehicle Turning Control.

_____ Notes _____

Chapter 6

Root Locus Method

6.1 Introduction

The relative stability of a control system is related to the location of the roots of the closed-loop characteristic equation. The transient response (i.e., settling time, overshoot, etc.) of a linear control system is also related to the location of the poles and zeros of the closed-loop transfer function. The closed-loop system relative stability and performance can sometimes be adjusted by changing a parameter, such as a control gain. The *root locus* method provides a *graphical* representation of the *locus* of roots of the characteristic equation as one parameter is varied. The graphical representation is called the *root locus plot*.

An approximate root locus sketch can be obtained by applying the orderly procedure outlined in *MCS, pp. 241-255*. Alternatively, we can use *MATLAB* to obtain an accurate root locus plot. However, do not be tempted to rely solely on *MATLAB* for obtaining root locus plots while neglecting the manual steps in developing an approximate root locus. The fundamental concepts behind the root locus method are buried in the manual steps and it is essential to fully understand their application.

The chapter begins with a discussion on obtaining a root locus plot with *MATLAB*. This is followed by a discussion of the connections between the partial fraction expansion, dominant poles, and the closed-loop system response. Root sensitivity is covered in the final section.

The functions covered in this chapter are **rlocus**, **rlocfind**, and **residue**. The functions **rlocus** and **rlocfind** are used to obtain root locus plots, and the **residue** function is utilized for partial fraction expansions of rational functions.

6.2   Obtaining a Root Locus Plot

Consider the closed-loop control system in Figure 6.1. The closed-loop transfer function is

$$T(s) = \frac{C(s)}{R(s)} = \frac{K(s+1)(s+3)}{s(s+2)(s+3) + K(s+1)}.$$

The characteristic equation can be written as

$$1 + K\frac{s+1}{s(s+2)(s+3)} = 0. \tag{6.1}$$

The form of the characteristic equation in Eq. (6.1) is necessary to use the **rlocus** function for generating root locus plots. The general form of the characteristic equation necessary for application of the **rlocus** function is

$$1 + k\frac{p(s)}{q(s)} = 0, \tag{6.2}$$

where k is the parameter of interest to be varied from $0 \leq k \leq \infty$. The **rlocus** function is shown in Figure 6.2. The steps to obtaining

Figure 6.1 Closed-Loop Control System with Unspecified Gain K.

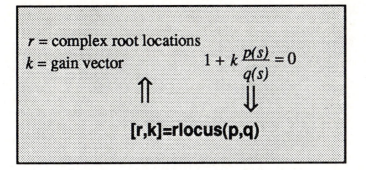

Figure 6.2 The **rlocus** Function.

the root locus plot associated with Eq. (6.1) are shown in Figure 6.3 along with the associated root locus plot. Invoking the **rlocus** function without left-hand arguments results in an automatic generation of the root locus plot. When invoked with left-hand arguments, the **rlocus** function returns a matrix of root locations and the associated gain vector.

The steps to obtain a root locus plot with *MATLAB* are as follows:

1. Obtain the characteristic equation in the form given in Eq. (6.2) where k is the parameter of interest, and
2. use the **rlocus** function to generate the plots.

Referring to Figure 6.3, we can see that as K increases, two branches of the root locus break away from the real axis. This means that for some values of K, the closed-loop system characteristic equation will have two complex roots. Suppose we want to find the value of K corresponding to a pair of complex roots. We can use the **rlocfind** function to do this, but only after a root locus has been obtained with the **rlocus** function. Executing the **rlocfind** function will result in a cross-hair marker appearing on the root-locus plot. You move the cross-hair marker to the location on the locus of interest and hit the enter key. The value of the parameter K and the selected point will then be displayed in the command display. The use of the **rlocfind** function is illustrated in Figure 6.4.

Continuing our third-order root locus example, we find that when $K = 20.5775$, the closed-loop transfer function has three poles and

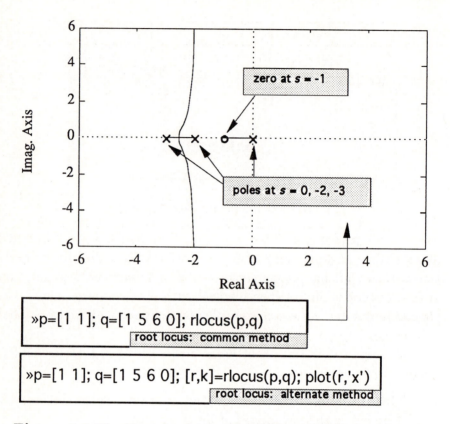

Figure 6.3 The Root Locus for the Characteristic Eq. (6.1).

two zeros at

$$\text{poles} : s = \begin{pmatrix} -2.0505 + 4.3227i \\ -2.0505 - 4.3227i \\ -.8989 \end{pmatrix} , \quad \text{zeros} : s = \begin{pmatrix} -1 \\ -3 \end{pmatrix}.$$

Considering the closed-loop pole locations only, we would expect that the real pole at $s = -.8989$ would be the *dominant* pole (see *MCS, p. 166*). To verify this, we can study the closed-loop system response to a step input, $R(s) = 1/s$. For a step input we have

$$C(s) = \frac{20.5775(s+1)(s+3)}{s(s+2)(s+3) + 20.5775(s+1)} \cdot \frac{1}{s}. \tag{6.3}$$

Generally, the first step in computing $c(t)$ is to expand Eq. (6.3) in a partial fraction expansion (see *MCS, pp. 45-52*). The **residue**

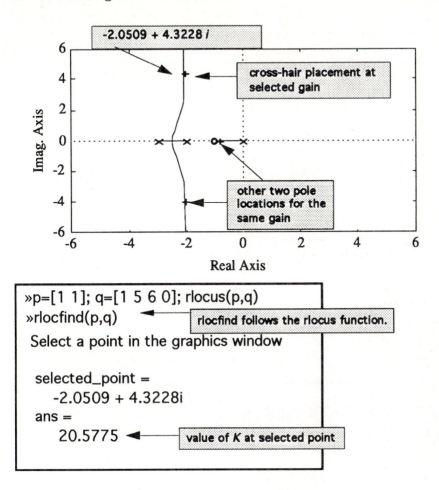

Figure 6.4 Using the **rlocfind** Function.

function can be used to expand Eq. (6.3), as shown in Figure 6.5. The **residue** function is described in Figure 6.6.

The partial fraction expansion of Eq. (6.3) is

$$C(s) = \frac{-1.3786 + 1.7010i}{s + 2.0505 + 4.3228i} + \frac{-1.3786 - 1.7010i}{s + 2.0505 - 4.3228i} + \frac{-0.2429}{s + 0.8989} + \frac{3}{s}.$$

Comparing the residues we see that the coefficient of the term corresponding to the pole at $s = -.8989$ is considerably smaller than the coefficient of the terms corresponding to the complex-conjugate poles at $s = -2.0505 \pm 4.3227i$. From this we expect that the influence of the pole at $s = -.8989$ on the output response $c(t)$ is

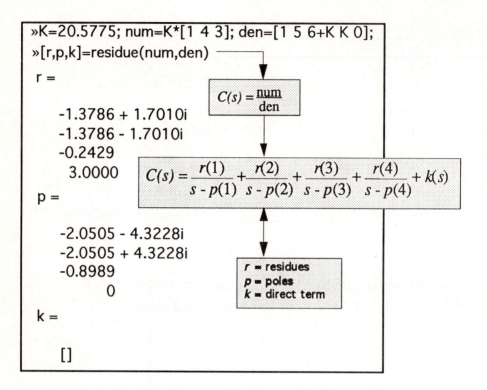

Figure 6.5 Partial Fraction Expansion of Eq. (6.3).

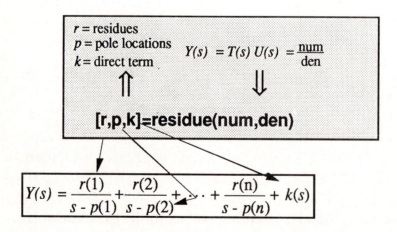

Figure 6.6 The **residue** Function.

not *dominant.* The settling time is then predicted by considering the complex-conjugate poles. The poles at $s = -2.0505 \pm 4.3227i$ correspond to a damping of $\zeta = 0.4286$ and a natural frequency of $\omega_n = 4.7844$. Thus, the settling time is predicted to be

$$T_s \approx \frac{4}{\zeta\omega_n} = 1.95 \text{ seconds.}$$

Using the **step** function, as shown in Figure 6.7, we find that $T_s \approx$ 1.6 seconds. So our approximation of settling time $T_s \approx 1.95$ is a fairly good good approximation. The percent overshoot is predicted to be

$$P.O. \approx 100 \exp^{-\zeta\pi/\sqrt{1-\zeta^2}} = 22.5\%.$$

As can be seen in Figure 6.7, the actual overshoot is very nearly 50%. Clearly, the prediction of overshoot is too low.

In this example the role of the system zeros on the transient response is illustrated. The proximity of the zero at $s = -1$ to the pole at $s = -0.8989$ reduces the impact of the pole on the transient

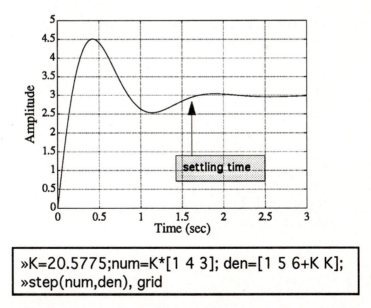

```
»K=20.5775;num=K*[1 4 3]; den=[1 5 6+K K];
»step(num,den), grid
```

Figure 6.7 Step Response for the Closed-Loop System in Figure 6.1 with $K = 20.5775$.

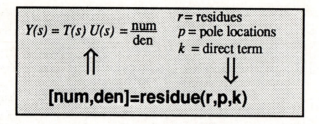

Figure 6.8 Converting a Partial Fraction Expansion Back to a Rational Function.

response. The main contributors to the transient response are the complex-conjugate poles at $s = -2.0505 \pm -4.3228i$.

One final point regarding the **residue** function. You can convert the partial fraction expansion back to the polynomials num/den, given the residues (r), the pole locations (p), and the direct terms (k), with the command shown in Figure 6.8.

6.3   Sensitivity and the Root Locus

The roots of the characteristic equation play an important role in defining the closed-loop system transient response. The effect of parameter variations on the roots of the characteristic equation is a useful measure of sensitivity. The root sensitivity can be defined to be

$$\frac{\partial r_i}{\partial k / k}. \tag{6.4}$$

We can utilize Eq. (6.4) to investigate the sensitivity of the roots of the characteristic equation to variations in the parameter k. If we change k by a small finite amount Δk, and evaluate the modified root $r_i + \Delta r_i$, it follows from Eq. (6.4) that

$$S_k^{r_i} = \frac{\Delta r_i}{\Delta k / k}. \tag{6.5}$$

The quantity $S_k^{r_i}$ is a complex number. Referring back to the third-order example in the previous section, if we change K a factor of 5%, we find that the dominant complex-conjugate pole at $s = -2.0505 + 4.3228i$ changes by

$$\Delta r_i = -0.0025 - 0.1168i$$

when K changes from $K = 20.5775$ to $K = 21.6064$. From Eq. (6.5), it follows that

$$S_k^{r_i} = \frac{-0.0025 - 0.1168i}{1.0289/20.5775} = -0.0494 - 2.3355i.$$

The sensitivity $S_k^{r_i}$ can also be written in the form

$$S_k^{r_i} = 2.3360 \;\; \angle 268.7872^\circ.$$

The magnitude and direction of $S_k^{r_i}$ provides a measure of the root sensitivity. The script used to perform the above sensitivity calculations is shown in Figure 6.9.

The root sensitivity measure may be useful for comparing the sensitivity for various system parameters at different root locations. However, the root sensitivity measure may not be that useful when utilized in the design process. It is primarily an analysis measure.

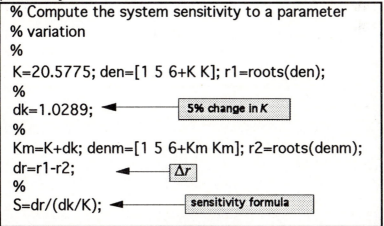

pfsensitivity.m

```
% Compute the system sensitivity to a parameter
% variation
%
K=20.5775; den=[1 5 6+K K]; r1=roots(den);
%
dk=1.0289;        ◄──────── 5% change in K
%
Km=K+dk; denm=[1 5 6+Km Km]; r2=roots(denm);
dr=r1-r2;         ◄──── Δr
%
S=dr/(dk/K);      ◄──────── sensitivity formula
```

Figure 6.9 Sensitivity Calculations for the Root Locus for a 5% Change in $K = 20.5775$.

_____ Notes _____

Chapter 7

Frequency Response Methods

7.1 Introduction

The frequency response of a system is the steady-state output response due to a sinusoidal input signal. In the previous chapters we have discussed the system response to various other test signals including steps, ramps, parabolas, and impulses. In this chapter, we will investigate the response of systems to sinusoidal inputs.

The frequency response methods are based on considering the response of linear systems to sinusoidal input test signals as the frequency of the sinusoidal test signal varies. A linear, time-invariant system has the characteristic that, in the steady-state, the output response due to a sinusoidal input differs from the input only in magnitude and phase. The transfer function describing the sinusoidal behavior of the system is obtained by replacing s with $j\omega$ in the system transfer function $G(s)$. Then, for a fixed ω, $G(j\omega)$ is a complex number with a magnitude and phase. The magnitude and phase of $G(j\omega)$ can be represented graphically as ω varies. This type of graphical representation is known as a *Bode diagram*. It is possible to develop control system performance specifications in the *frequency domain* so that an effective control system design methodology using the Bode diagram can be used.

The chapter begins with an introduction to the Bode diagram. Subsequently, the connection between the frequency response and performance specifications in the time-domain is discussed. The chapter concludes with an illustrative example to gain experience designing a control system in the frequency domain.

The functions covered are **bode** and **logspace**. The **bode** function is used to generate a Bode diagram, and the **logspace** function generates a logarithmically spaced vector of frequencies utilized by the **bode** function.

7.2   Bode Diagram

Suppose we have the transfer function (see *MCS, p. 321*)

$$G(s) = \frac{5(1 + 0.1s)}{s(1 + 0.5s)(1 + \frac{0.6}{50}s + \frac{1}{50^2}s^2)}. \tag{7.1}$$

The Bode diagram corresponding to Eq. (7.1) is shown in Figure 7.1. The diagram consists of the logarithmic gain in dB versus ω in one plot and the phase $\phi(\omega)$ versus ω in a second plot. The manual steps for sketching an approximate Bode diagram are given in *MCS, pp. 308-317*. As with the root locus plots, it will be tempting to rely exclusively on *MATLAB* to obtain your Bode diagrams. Treat *MATLAB* as one tool in your tool kit that you can use to design and

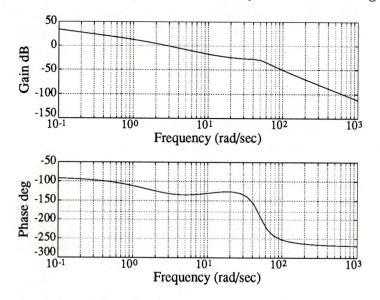

Figure 7.1 The Bode Plot Associated with Eq. (7.1).

analyze control systems. It is essential to develop the capability to manually obtain approximate Bode diagrams. There is no substitute for a clear understanding of the underlying theory.

A Bode diagram is obtained with the **bode** function shown in Figure 7.2. The Bode diagram is automatically generated if the **bode** function is invoked without left-hand arguments. Otherwise, the magnitude and phase characteristics are placed in the workspace through the variables mag and phase. A Bode diagram is obtained with the **plot** function using mag, phase, and ω. The vector ω contains the values of the frequency in radians/sec at which the Bode diagram will be calculated. If ω is not specified, *MATLAB* will automatically choose the frequency values by placing more points in regions where the frequency response is changing quickly. Since the Bode diagram is a log scale, if you choose to specify the frequencies explicitly, it is desirable to generate the vector ω using the **logspace** function. The **logspace** function is shown in Figure 7.3.

The Bode diagram in Figure 7.1 is generated with the commands shown in Figure 7.4. The **bode** function automatically selected the

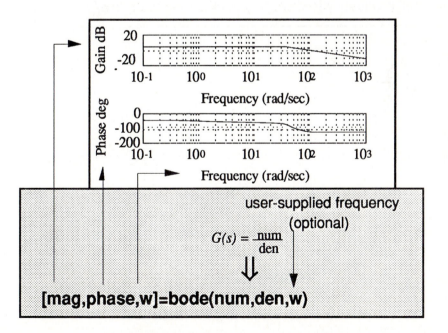

Figure 7.2 The **bode** Function.

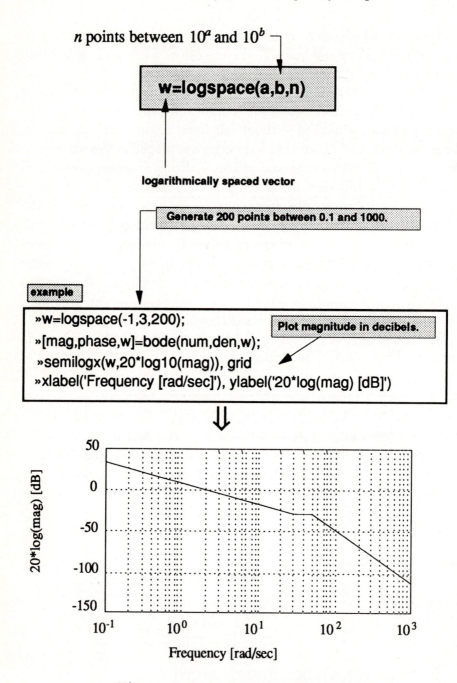

Figure 7.3 The **logspace** Function.

bodescript.m

```
% Bode plot script for Figure 7.21 in MCS, p. 324
%
num=5*[0.1 1];
f1=[1 0]; f2=[0.5 1]; f3=[1/2500 .6/50 1];
den=conv(f1,conv(f2,f3));
%
bode(num,den)
```

compute
$$s(1+0.5s)(1+\frac{0.6}{50}s+\frac{1}{50^2}s^2)$$

Figure 7.4 The Script for the Bode Diagram in Figure 7.1.

frequency range as $\omega = 0.1$ to 1000 rad/sec. This range is user-selectable with the **logspace** function.

7.3 Specifications in the Frequency Domain

Keeping in mind our goal of designing control systems that satisfy certain performance specifications given in the time-domain, we must establish a connection between the frequency response and the transient time response of a system. The relationship between specifications given in the time domain to those given in the frequency domain depend upon approximation of the system by a second-order system with the poles being the system *dominant roots*. This approximation is discussed in *MCS, pp. 241-255*.

Consider the second-order system shown in Figure 7.5. The

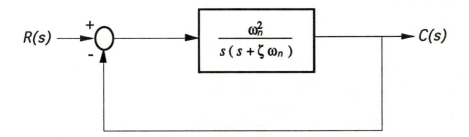

Figure 7.5 Single-Loop Second-Order Feedback System.

closed-loop transfer function is

$$T(s) = \frac{\omega_n^2}{s^2 + 2\zeta\omega_n s + \omega_n^2}.$$ (7.2)

The Bode diagram magnitude characteristics associated with the closed-loop transfer function in Eq. (7.2) are shown in Figure 7.6. The relationship between the resonant frequency, ω_r, the maximum of the frequency response, M_{p_ω}, and the damping ratio, ζ, and the natural frequency, ω_n, is shown in Figure 7.7 (and in Figure 7.10 in *MCS, p.316*). The information in Figure 7.7 will be quite helpful in designing control systems in the frequency domain while satisfying time-domain specifications.

We have seen that we can relate frequency-domain specifications to time-domain specifications by using the information contained in

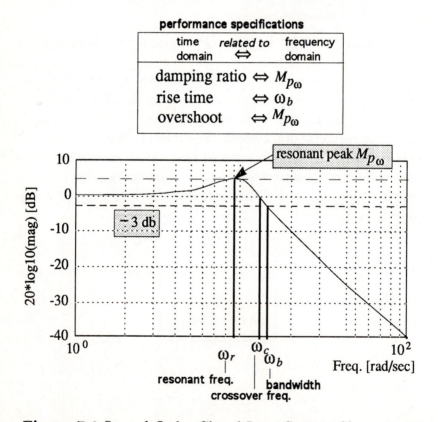

Figure 7.6 Second-Order Closed-Loop System Characteristics.

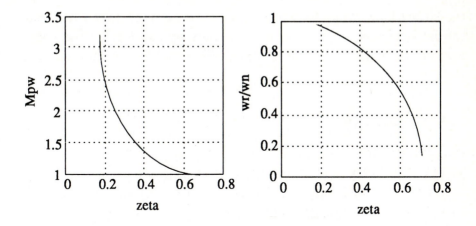

relation.m

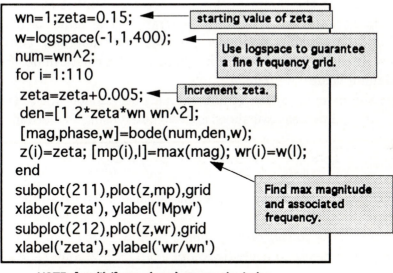

```
wn=1;zeta=0.15;          ◄──── starting value of zeta
w=logspace(-1,1,400);    ◄──
num=wn^2;                      Use logspace to guarantee
                               a fine frequency grid.
for i=1:110
  zeta=zeta+0.005;  ◄──┤ Increment zeta.
  den=[1 2*zeta*wn wn^2];
  [mag,phase,w]=bode(num,den,w);
  z(i)=zeta; [mp(i),l]=max(mag); wr(i)=w(l);
end
                               Find max magnitude
subplot(211),plot(z,mp),grid   and associated
xlabel('zeta'), ylabel('Mpw')  frequency.
subplot(212),plot(z,wr),grid
xlabel('zeta'), ylabel('wr/wn')
```

NOTE: [mp(l),l]=max(mag) stores the index
of the maximum mag in the variable l.

Figure 7.7 The Relationship Between (M_{p_ω}, ω_r) and (ζ, ω_n) for a Second-Order System.

the closed-loop Bode diagram. Stability is an important issue that can be addressed in the frequency domain by considering the *open-loop* transfer function. This topic will be addressed in the next chapter.

7.4   Example: Engraving Machine System

Consider the block diagram model in Figure 7.8. This example can be found in *MCS, pp. 332-335*. Our objective is to design K so that the closed-loop system has an acceptable time response to a step command. A functional block diagram describing the frequency domain design process is shown in Figure 7.9. First we choose $K = 2$ and subsequently iterate on K if the performance is unacceptable. A script, shown in Figure 7.10, is used in the design. The value of K is defined at the command level. Then the script is executed and the closed-loop Bode diagram is generated. The values of $M_{p\omega}$ and ω_r are determined by inspection from the Bode diagram. Those values are used in conjunction with Figure 7.7 to determine the corresponding values of ζ and ω_n.

Given the damping ratio, ζ, and the natural frequency, ω_n, the settling time and percent overshoot are estimated using the formulas

$$T_s \approx \frac{4}{\zeta \omega_n} \, , \quad P.O. \approx 100 \exp \frac{-\zeta \pi}{\sqrt{1 - \zeta^2}}.$$

If the time-domain specifications are not satisfied, then we adjust K and iterate.

The values for ζ and ω_n corresponding to $K = 2$ are $\zeta = 0.29$ and $\omega_n = 0.88$. This leads to a prediction of $P.O. = 38\%$ and $T_s = 16$

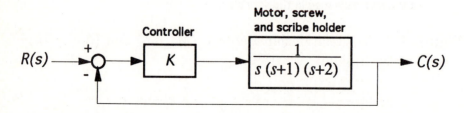

Figure 7.8 Engraving Machine Block Diagram Model.

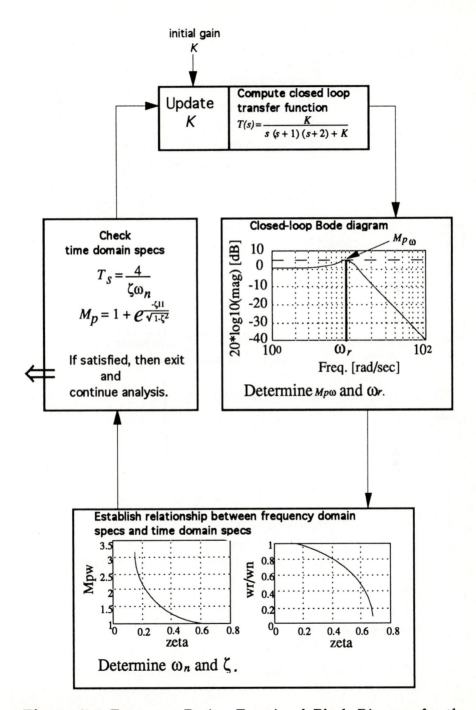

Figure 7.9 Frequency Design Functional Block Diagram for the Engraving Machine.

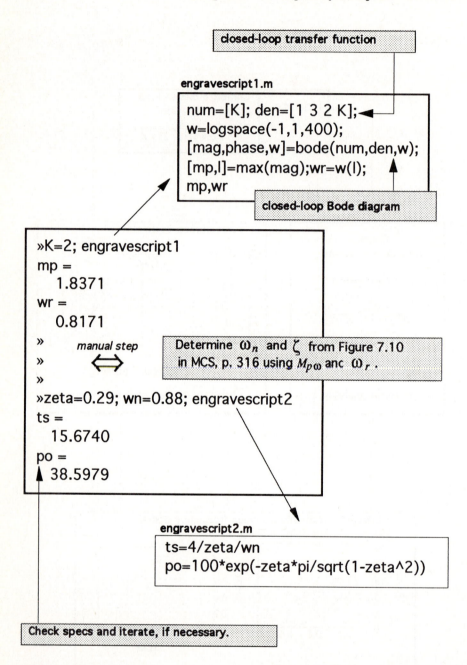

Figure 7.10 Frequency Design Script for the Engraving Machine.

seconds. The step response, shown in Figure 7.11, is a verification that the performance predictions are quite accurate and the closed-loop system performs adequately.

In this example, the second-order system approximation is reasonable and leads to an acceptable design. However, the second-order approximation may not always lead directly to a good design. Fortunately, with *MATLAB* we have the possibility to construct an interactive design facility that can assist us in the design process by reducing the manual computational loads while providing easy access to a host of classical and modern control tools.

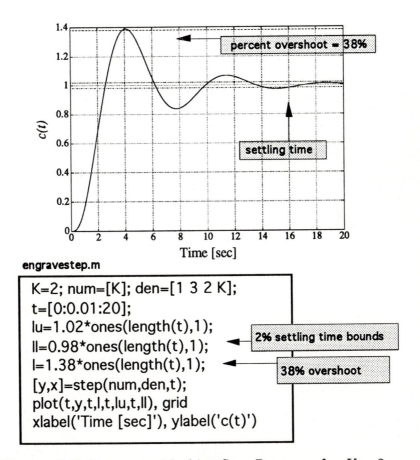

```
K=2; num=[K]; den=[1 3 2 K];
t=[0:0.01:20];
lu=1.02*ones(length(t),1);
ll=0.98*ones(length(t),1);
l=1.38*ones(length(t),1);
[y,x]=step(num,den,t);
plot(t,y,t,l,t,lu,t,ll), grid
xlabel('Time [sec]'), ylabel('c(t)')
```

Figure 7.11 Engraving Machine Step Response for $K = 2$.

_____ Notes _____

Chapter 8

Stability in the Frequency Domain

8.1　Introduction

Stability of a control system can be determined with frequency-response methods. The basis for the frequency-domain stability analysis is the *Nyquist stability criterion*. Issues of absolute stability as well as relative stability can be addressed in the frequency domain. Graphical methods play an important role in the frequency-domain design and analysis of control systems. We will utilize several frequency-domain plots in our stability investigations, and, of course, we will use *MATLAB* to aid in obtaining our plots.

The chapter begins with a discussion of the Nyquist stability criterion and the *Nyquist* diagram and *Nichols* chart. We will also revisit the Bode diagram in our discussions on relative stability. Two examples are given which illustrate the frequency-domain design approach. We will make use of the frequency response of the closed-loop transfer function, $T(j\omega)$, as well as the loop transfer function $GH(j\omega)$. We present an illustrative example that shows how to deal with a time delay in the system by utilizing a Padé approximation.

The functions covered in this chapter are **nyquist, nichols, margin, pade,** and **ngrid**.

103

8.2   Nyquist Plots

The Nyquist stability criterion is based on Cauchy's theorem, which is concerned with mapping contours in the complex s-plane. Consider the system in Figure 8.1. The closed-loop transfer function is

$$T(s) = \frac{G(s)}{1 + GH(s)},$$

and the characteristic equation is

$$F(s) = 1 + GH(s) = 0.$$

All of the zeroes of $F(s)$ must lie in the left-hand s-plane for stability. We choose a contour, Γ_s, in the s-plane which encloses the entire right-hand s-plane, and plot Γ_F in the $F(s)$-plane and determine the number of encirclements of the origin. Equivalently, we can plot Γ_P in the $P(s)$-plane and determine the number of encirclements of the -1 point, where $P(s) = F(s) - 1$. The Nyquist stability criterion can be stated as follows:

> A feedback control system is stable if and only if, for the contours Γ_P, the number of counterclockwise encirclements of the $(-1, 0)$ point is equal to the number of poles of $P(s)$ with positive real parts (see *MCS, p. 362*).

The plot of Γ_P is the Nyquist plot. It is generally more difficult to

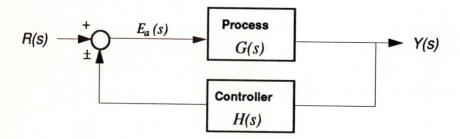

Figure 8.1 Single-Loop Feedback Control System.

generate the Nyquist plot manually than the Bode diagram. However, we can use *MATLAB* to generate the Nyquist plot rather easily.

The Nyquist plot is generated with the **nyquist** function, as shown in Figure 8.2. When **nyquist** is used without left-hand arguments, the Nyquist plot is automatically generated; otherwise, you must use the **plot** function to generate the plot using the vectors re and im.

One cautionary remark regarding Nyquist plots: Some time in the course of using the **nyquist** function you may find that your Nyquist plot looks strange or that some information appears to be missing. It may be necessary in these cases to use the **axis** function to override the automatic scaling and use the **nyquist** function with left-hand arguments in conjunction with the **plot** function. In this way you can focus in on the −1 point region for your stability analysis, as illustrated in Figure 8.3.

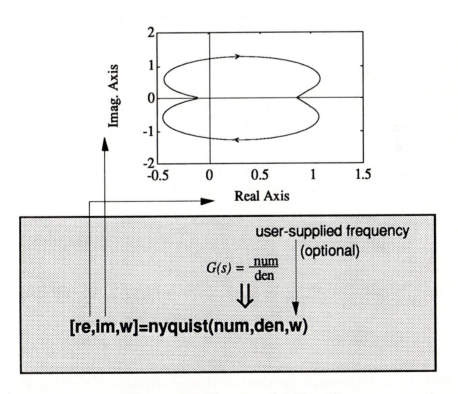

Figure 8.2 The **nyquist** Function.

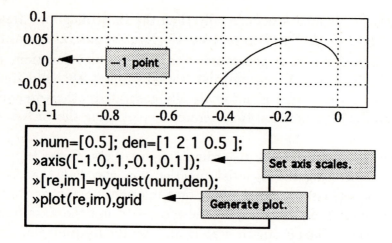

```
»num=[0.5]; den=[1 2 1 0.5 ];
»axis([-1.0,.1,-0.1,0.1]);      ◄── Set axis scales.
»[re,im]=nyquist(num,den);
»plot(re,im),grid      ◄── Generate plot.
```

Figure 8.3 The **nyquist** Function with Manual Scaling.

Up to this point we have been considering absolute stability only. In other words, our concern has been whether a system is stable or not. However, relative stability measures of *gain* and *phase* margins can be determined from both the Nyquist plot and the Bode diagram. The gain margin is a measure of how much the system gain would have to be increased for the $GH(j\omega)$ locus to pass through the $(-1,0)$ point, thus resulting in an unstable system. The phase margin is a measure of the additional phase lag required before the system becomes unstable. Gain and phase margins can be determined from both the Nyquist plot and the Bode diagram.

Consider the system shown in Figure 8.4. Relative stability can

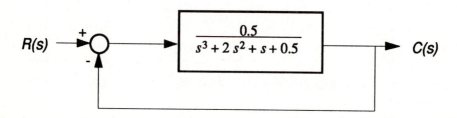

Figure 8.4 A Closed-Loop Control System Example for Nyquist and Bode with Relative Stability.

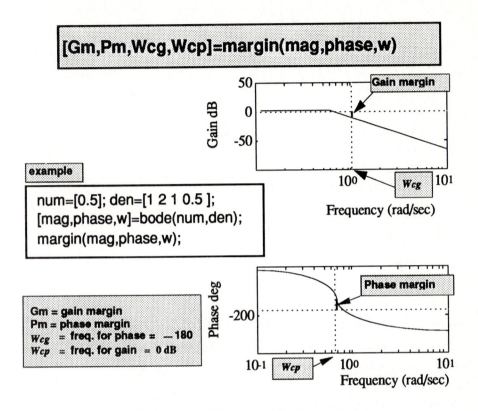

Figure 8.5 The **margin** Function.

be determined from the Bode diagram using the **margin** function. The **margin** function is invoked in conjunction with the **bode** function to compute the gain and phase margins. The **margin** function is shown in Figure 8.5. If the **margin** function is invoked without left-hand arguments, the Bode diagram is automatically generated with the gain and phase margins labeled on the diagram. This is illustrated in Figure 8.6 for the system that is shown in Figure 8.4.

The script to generate the Nyquist plot for the system in Figure 8.4 is shown in Figure 8.7. In this case, the number of poles of $GH(s)$ with positive real parts is zero and the number of counter-clockwise encirclements of -1 is zero; hence the closed-loop system is stable. We can also determine the gain and phase margins, as indicated in Figure 8.7.

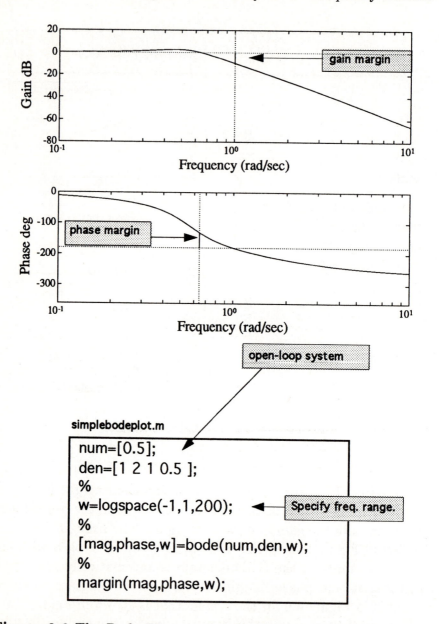

Figure 8.6 The Bode Diagram for the System in Figure 8.4 with Gain and Phase Margins.

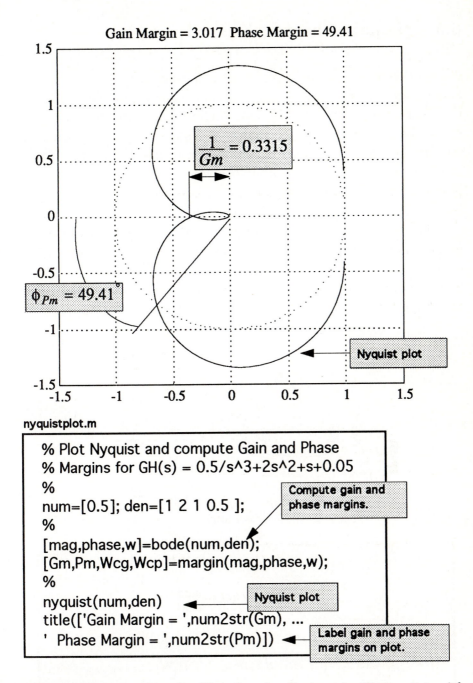

Figure 8.7 The Nyquist Plot for the System in Figure 8.4 with Gain and Phase Margins.

8.3   Nichols Charts

Another frequency-domain plot that can be used in the design and analysis of control systems is the Nichols chart. The Nichols chart is discussed in *MCS, pp. 378-386*. Nichols charts can be generated using the **nichols** function, shown in Figure 8.8. If the **nichols** function is invoked without left-hand arguments, the Nichols chart is automatically generated, otherwise you must use **nichols** in conjunction with the **plot** function. A Nichols chart grid is drawn on the existing plot with the **ngrid** function.

The **margin** function works best in conjunction with the **bode** function. It is possible to use the **margin** function after executing **nichols** but, unless you desire a Bode plot with gain and phase margin labels, you should invoke **margin** with left-hand arguments and place the gain and phase margin values in the workspace. The

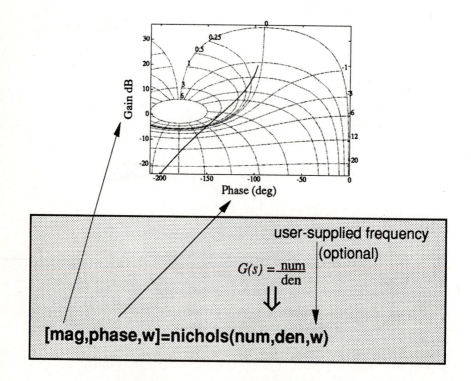

Figure 8.8 The **nichols** Function.

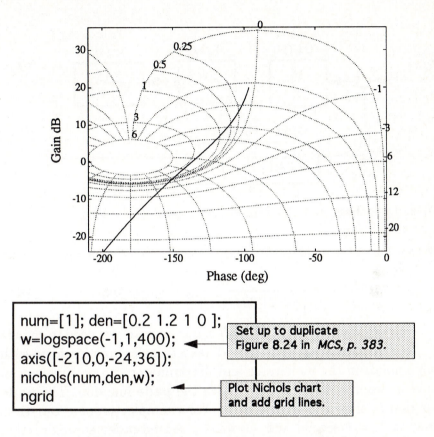

Figure 8.9 code box:
```
num=[1]; den=[0.2 1.2 1 0 ];
w=logspace(-1,1,400);
axis([-210,0,-24,36]);
nichols(num,den,w);
ngrid
```

Set up to duplicate
Figure 8.24 in *MCS, p. 383.*

Plot Nichols chart
and add grid lines.

Figure 8.9 Nichols Chart for Eq. (8.1).

Nichols chart, shown in Figure 8.9, is for the system

$$G(j\omega) = \frac{1}{j\omega(j\omega + 1)(0.2j\omega + 1)}. \qquad (8.1)$$

8.4 Examples

■ EXAMPLE 8.1 Liquid Level Control System

Consider a liquid level control system described by the block diagram shown in Figure 8.10 (see *MCS, pp. 387-388*). Notice that this

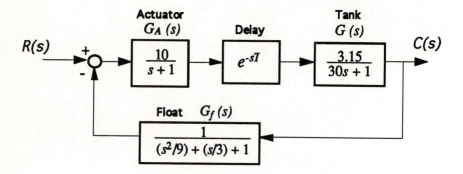

Figure 8.10 Liquid Level Control System.

system has a time delay. The loop transfer function is given by

$$GH(s) = \frac{31.5}{(s+1)(30s+1)(\frac{s^2}{9} + \frac{s}{3} + 1)} \exp^{-sT} . \qquad (8.2)$$

Since we want to use *MATLAB* in our analysis, we need to change Eq. (8.2) in such a way that $GH(s)$ has a transfer function form with polynomials in the numerator and denominator. To do this we can make an approximation to e^{-sT} with the **pade** function. The **pade** function is shown in Figure 8.11. For example, suppose our time delay is $T = 1$ second and we want a second-order approximation $n = 2$. Then, using the **pade** function we find that

$$e^{-s} \approx \frac{0.0743s^2 - 0.4460s + 0.8920}{0.0743s^2 + 0.4460s + 0.8920}. \qquad (8.3)$$

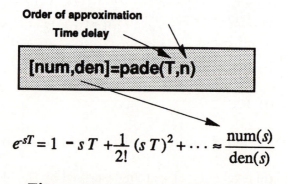

Figure 8.11 The **pade** Function.

Substituting Eq. (8.3) into Eq. (8.2) we have

$$GH(s) \approx \frac{31.5(0.0743s^2 - 0.4460s + 0.8920)}{(s+1)(30s+1)(\frac{s^2}{9} + \frac{s}{3} + 1)(0.0743s^2 + 0.4460s + 0.8920)}$$

Now we can build a script to investigate the relative stability of the system using the Bode diagram. Our goal is to have a phase margin of 30 degrees. The associated script is shown in Figure 8.12. To make the script interactive, we let the gain K (now set at $K = 31.5$) be variable and defined outside the script at the command level. Then we set K and run the script to check the phase margin and iterate if necessary. The final selected gain is $K = 16$. Remember that we have utilized a second-order Padé approximation of the time delay in our analysis.

■ **EXAMPLE 8.2 Remote Controlled Battlefield Vehicle**

Consider the speed control system for a remotely controlled battlefield vehicle shown in Figure 8.13 (see *MCS, pp. 392-402*). The design objective is to achieve good control with low steady-state error and low overshoot to a step command. We will build a script to allow us to perform many design iterations quickly and efficiently. First, let's investigate the steady-state error specification. The steady-state error, e_{ss}, to a unit step command is

$$e_{ss} = \frac{1}{1 + K/2}. \tag{8.4}$$

The effect of the gain K on the steady-state error is clear from Eq. (8.4). If $K = 20$, the error is 9% of the input magnitude. If $K = 10$, the error is 17% of the input magnitude, and so on.

Now we can investigate the overshoot specification in the frequency domain. Suppose we demand that the percent overshoot be less than 50%. Solving

$$P.O. \approx 100 \exp^{-\zeta\pi/\sqrt{1-\zeta^2}} \leq 50$$

for ζ yields

$$\zeta \geq 0.215.$$

Referring to Figure 7.7 (or *MCS, p.316*) we find that $M_{p\omega} \leq 2.45$.

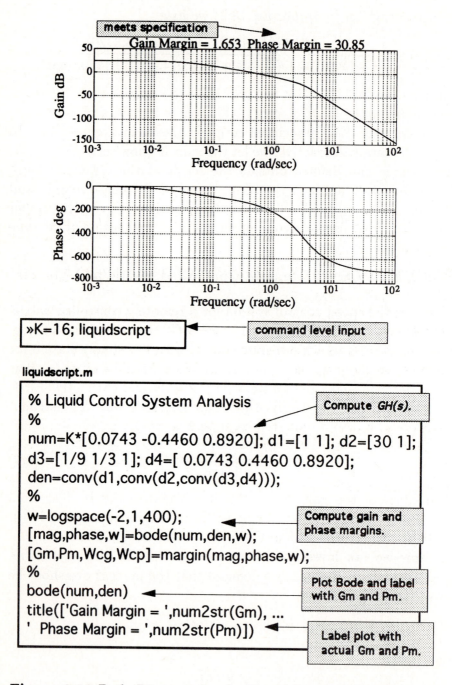

Figure 8.12 Bode Diagram for the Liquid Level Control System.

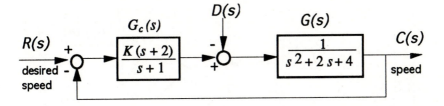

Figure 8.13 Battlefield Vehicle Speed Control System.

We must keep in mind that the information in Figure 7.7 is for second-order systems only and can be used here only as a guideline. We now compute the closed-loop Bode diagram and check the values of $M_{p\omega}$. Any gain K for which $M_{p\omega} \leq 2.45$ may be a valid gain for our design, but we will have to investigate further to include step responses to check the actual overshoot. The script in Figure 8.14 aids us in this task. In keeping with the spirit of the design steps in *MCS, pp. 392-402*, we investigate further the gains $K = 20, 10$, and 4.44 (even though $M_{p\omega} > 2.45$ for $K = 20$). We can plot the step responses to quantify the overshoot, as shown in Figure 8.15.

Alternately, we could have used a Nichols chart to aid the design process. This is shown in Figure 8.16.

The results of the analysis are summarized in Table 8.1 for $K = 20, 10$, and 4.44. Suppose we choose $K = 10$ as our design gain. Then we obtain the Nyquist plot and check relative stability. This is shown in Figure 8.17. The gain margin is $GM = 49.56$ and the phase margin is $PM = 26.11°$.

Table 8.1 Actual Response for Selected Gains.

K	4.44	10	20
Percent overshoot	5%	30%	50%
Settling time	3.5	5	6
Peak time	1.4	1.0	0.7
e_{ss}	31%	17%	9%

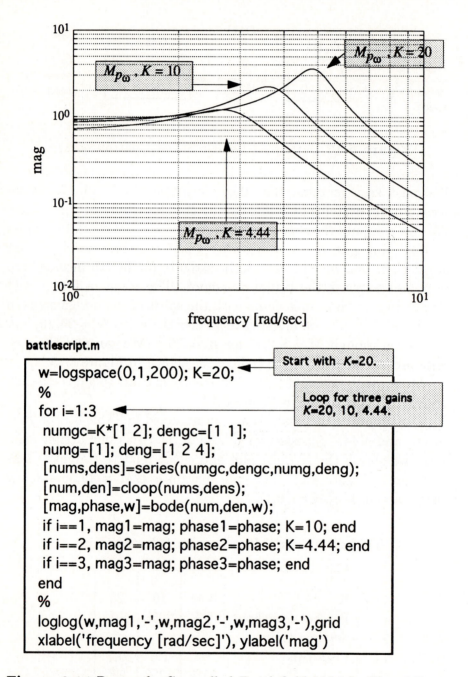

Figure 8.14 Remotely Controlled Battlefield Vehicle Closed-Loop System Bode Diagram Script.

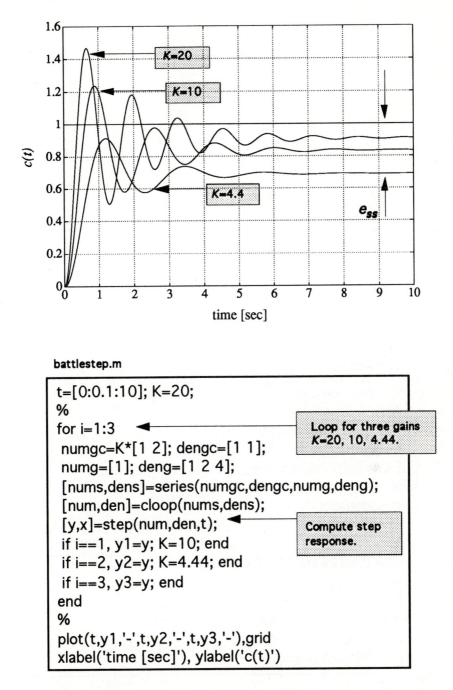

Figure 8.15 Remotely Controlled Battlefield Vehicle Step Response.

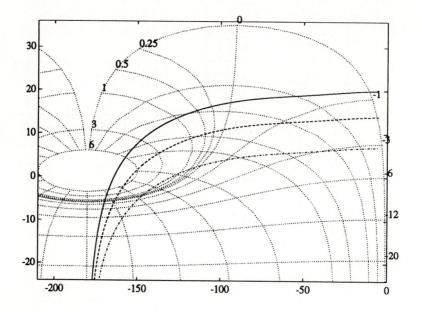

battlenichols.m

```
% Remotely Controlled Battlefield Vehicle
%
numgc=[1 2]; dengc=[1 1];
numg=[1]; deng=[1 2 4];              Compute GcG(s).
[num,den]=series(numgc,dengc,numg,deng);
%
w=logspace(-1,2,200);                Set up plot to match
axis([-210,0,-24,36])                Figure 8.32 in MCS, p. 394.
%
K1=20; K2=10; K3=4.44;               Nichols chart for
[mag1,ph1,w]=nichols(K1*num,den,w);  K=20,10,4.44.
[mag2,ph2,w]=nichols(K2*num,den,w);
[mag3,ph3,w]=nichols(K3*num,den,w);
plot(ph1,20*log10(mag1),'-',ph2,20*log10(mag2),'--',...
ph3,20*log10(mag3),'-.'),ngrid
```

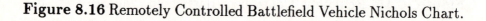

Figure 8.16 Remotely Controlled Battlefield Vehicle Nichols Chart.

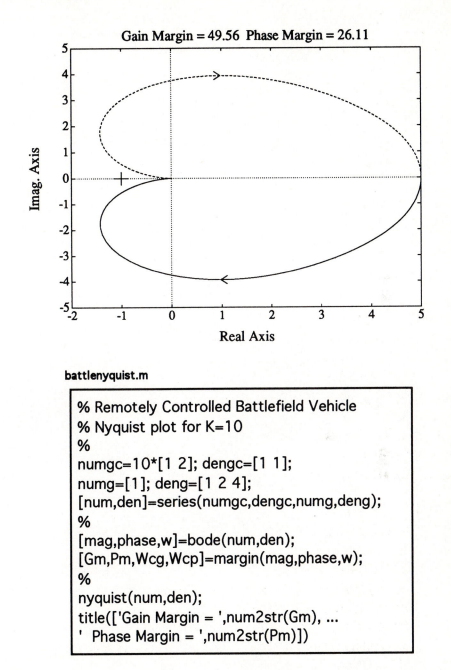

Figure 8.17 Nyquist Chart for the Remotely Controlled Battlefield Vehicle with $K = 10$.

_____ Notes _____

Chapter 9

State-Space Methods

9.1 Introduction

In the previous chapters we considered control system design and analysis in the frequency domain. We utilized the Laplace transform to transform the linear, constant coefficient differential equation model into an algebraic expression in terms of the complex variable s. Then we operated on our system in input-output (or transfer function) form

$$C(s) = \frac{b_m s^m + \cdots + b_1 s + b_0}{s^n + a_{n-1} s^{n-1} + \cdots + a_1 s + a_0} R(s) = G(s) R(s).$$

In this chapter we begin to look at control system design and analysis in the time domain. In contrast to the frequency-domain approach, the time-domain method utilizes a *state-space* representation of the system model, given by

$$\begin{aligned} \dot{\boldsymbol{x}} &= \boldsymbol{A}\boldsymbol{x} + \boldsymbol{B}u \\ c &= \boldsymbol{D}\boldsymbol{x} + \boldsymbol{H}u \end{aligned} \tag{9.1}$$

The vector $\boldsymbol{x}$ is the *state* of the system, $\boldsymbol{A}$ is the constant $n \times n$ system matrix, $\boldsymbol{B}$ is the constant $n \times m$ input matrix, $\boldsymbol{D}$ is the constant $p \times n$ output matrix and $\boldsymbol{H}$ is a constant $p \times m$ matrix. The number of inputs, m, and the number of outputs, p, are taken to be one since we are considering only single-input, single-output problems. Therefore c and u are not bold variables.

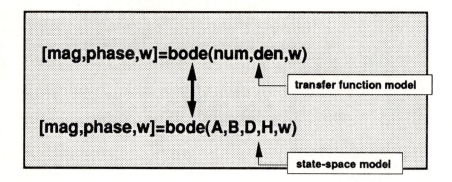

Figure 9.1 The State-Space Representation **bode** Function.

The main elements of the state-space representation in Eq. (9.1) are the state vector x and the constant matrices (A, B, D, H). Since the main computational unit in *MATLAB* is the matrix, the state-space representation lends itself well to the *MATLAB* environment. In fact, *MATLAB* covers so many aspects of state-space methods that we will not be able to discuss them all here.

The new functions covered in this chapter are **tf2ss** and **ss2tf**. Most of the functions covered in the previous chapters also apply here. For example, the the **bode** function can be utilized with a state-space model, as shown in Figure 9.1. The same idea applies to **series, parallel, feedback, cloop, printsys, minreal, step, pzmap, impulse, lsim, rlocus, rlocfind, residue, bode, nyquist,** and **nichols.**

9.2   Model Relationships

Given a transfer function we can obtain an equivalent state-space representation, and vice versa. *MATLAB* has two functions that convert systems from transfer function to state space and back. The function **tf2ss** converts a transfer-function representation to a state-space representation; the function **ss2tf** converts a state-space representation to a transfer function. These functions are shown in Figure 9.2.

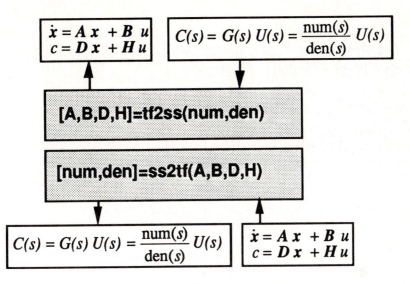

Figure 9.2 Linear System Model Conversion.

For instance, consider the third-order system

$$T(s) = \frac{C(s)}{R(s)} = \frac{2s^2 + 8s + 6}{s^3 + 8s^2 + 16s + 6}. \tag{9.2}$$

We can obtain a state-space representation using the **tf2ss** function as shown in Figure 9.3. The state-space representation of Eq. (9.2) is given by Eq. (9.1) where

$$A = \begin{bmatrix} -8 & -16 & -6 \\ 1 & 0 & 0 \\ 0 & 1 & 0 \end{bmatrix}, \quad B = \begin{bmatrix} 1 \\ 0 \\ 0 \end{bmatrix},$$

and

$$D = \begin{bmatrix} 2 & 8 & 6 \end{bmatrix}, \quad H = [0].$$

Notice that the **printsys** function lists the system matrices as a, b, c, d. The conversion to our notation is as follows:

$$a \mapsto A, \quad b \mapsto B, \quad c \mapsto D, \quad d \mapsto H.$$

convert.m

```
% Convert G(s) = (2s^2+8s+6)/(s^3+8s^2+16s+6)
% to a state-space representation
%
num=[2 8 6]; den=[1 8 16 6];
[A,B,D,H]=tf2ss(num,den);
printsys(A,B,D,H)
```

»convert

a =

	x1	x2	x3
x1	-8.00000	-16.00000	-6.00000
x2	1.00000	0	0
x3	0	1.00000	0

b =

	u1
x1	1.00000
x2	0
x3	0

c =

	x1	x2	x3
y1	2.00000	8.00000	6.00000

d =

	u1
y1	0

Figure 9.3 Conversion of Eq. (9.2) to a State-Space Representation.

9.3 Stability of Systems in the Time Domain

Suppose we have a system in state-space form as in Eq. (9.1). The stability of the system can be evaluated with the *characteristic equation* associated with the system matrix $\boldsymbol{A}$. The characteristic equation is

$$\det(s\boldsymbol{I} - \boldsymbol{A}) = 0. \tag{9.3}$$

The characteristic equation is a polynomial in s. If all of the roots of the characteristic equation have negative real parts (i.e., $Re(s_i) < 0, \forall i$), then the system is stable.

When the system model is given in the state-space form we must calculate the characteristic polynomial associated with the $\boldsymbol{A}$ matrix. In this regard we have several options. We can calculate the characteristic equation directly from Eq. (9.3) by manually computing the determinant of $(s\boldsymbol{I} - \boldsymbol{A})$. Then we can compute the roots using the **roots** function to check for stability, or alternatively, we can utilize the Routh-Hurwitz method to detect any unstable roots. Unfortunately, the manual computations can become lengthy, especially if the dimension of $\boldsymbol{A}$ is large. We would like to avoid this manual computation if possible. As it turns out, *MATLAB* can assist in this endeavor.

The **poly** function described in Chapter 2 can be used to compute the characteristic equation associated with $\boldsymbol{A}$. Recall that **poly** is used to form a polynomial from a vector of roots. It can also be used to compute the characteristic equation of $\boldsymbol{A}$, as illustrated in Figure 9.4, wherein input matrix, $\boldsymbol{A}$, is

$$\boldsymbol{A} = \begin{bmatrix} -8 & -16 & -6 \\ 1 & 0 & 0 \\ 0 & 1 & 0 \end{bmatrix}$$

and the associated characteristic polynomial is

$$s^3 + 8s^2 + 16s + 6.$$

If $\boldsymbol{A}$ is an $n \times n$ matrix, **poly($\boldsymbol{A}$)** is the characteristic equation represented by the $n+1$ element row vector whose elements are the coefficients of the characteristic equation.

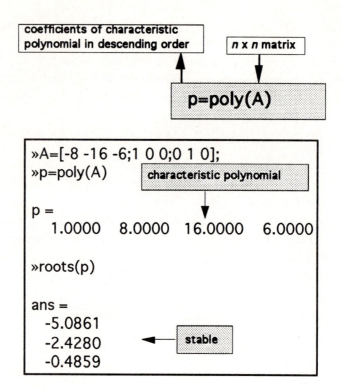

Figure 9.4 Computing the Characteristic Equation of **A** with the
poly Function.

■ EXAMPLE 9.1 Automatic Test System

The state-space representation for the automatic test system (see
MCS, pp. 462-465) is

$$\dot{x} = Ax + Bu \qquad (9.4)$$

where

$$A = \begin{bmatrix} 0 & 1 & 0 \\ 0 & -1 & 1 \\ 0 & 0 & -5 \end{bmatrix}, \quad B = \begin{bmatrix} 0 \\ 0 \\ K \end{bmatrix}.$$

Our design specifications are (i) step response with a settling time
less than two seconds, and (ii) overshoot less than 4%. We assume
that the state variables are available for feedback so that the control

is given by

$$u = (-K_1, -K_2, -K_3)\, \boldsymbol{x}. \tag{9.5}$$

We must select the gains K, K_1, K_2 and K_3 to meet the performance specifications. Using the design approximation

$$T_s \approx \frac{4}{\zeta\omega_n} < 2 \quad \text{and} \quad P.O. \approx 100\exp^{-\zeta\pi/\sqrt{1-\zeta^2}} < 4,$$

we find that

$$\zeta > 0.72 \quad \text{and} \quad \omega_n > 2.8.$$

This defines a region in the complex plane in which our dominant roots must lie to have any chance of meeting the design specifications. Substituting Eq. (9.5) into Eq. (9.4) yields

$$\dot{\boldsymbol{x}} = \begin{bmatrix} 0 & 1 & 0 \\ 0 & -1 & 1 \\ -KK_1 & -KK_2 & -(5+KK_3) \end{bmatrix} \boldsymbol{x} = \boldsymbol{A}^*\boldsymbol{x}, \tag{9.6}$$

where $\boldsymbol{A}^*$ is the revised $\boldsymbol{A}$ matrix. The characteristic equation associated with Eq. (9.6) can be obtained by evaluating $det(s\boldsymbol{I}-\boldsymbol{A}^*) = 0$. This results in

$$s(s+1)(s+5) + KK_3\left(s^2 + \frac{K_3+K_2}{K_3}s + \frac{K_1}{K_3}\right) = 0. \tag{9.7}$$

If we view KK_3 as a parameter and let $K_1 = 1$, then we can write Eq. (9.7) as follows:

$$1 + KK_3\frac{s^2 + \frac{K_3+K_2}{K_3}s + \frac{1}{K_3}}{s(s+1)(s+5)} = 0.$$

We place the zeros at $s = -4 \pm 2j$ in order to pull the locus to the left in the s-plane. Thus our desired numerator polynomial is $s^2 + 8s + 20$. Comparing corresponding coefficients leads to

$$\frac{K_3+K_2}{K_3} = 8 \quad \text{and} \quad \frac{1}{K_3} = 20.$$

Therefore $K_2 = 0.35$ and $K_3 = 0.05$. We can now plot a root locus with KK_3 as the parameter, as shown in Figure 9.5. The

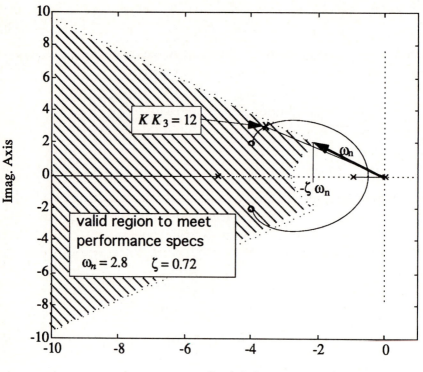

```
autolocus.m
% Root locus script for the Automatic Test System
% including performance specs regions
num=[1 8 20]; den=[1 6 5 0];
clg; rlocus(num,den); hold on  ◄────  Hold plot to add
%                                      stability regions.
zeta=0.72; wn=2.8;
x=[-10:0.1:-zeta*wn]; y=-(sqrt(1-zeta^2)/zeta)*x;
xc=[-10:0.1:-zeta*wn];c=sqrt(wn^2-xc.^2);
plot(x,y,':',x,-y,':',xc,c,':',xc,-c,':')
```

Figure 9.5 Root Locus for the Automatic Test System.

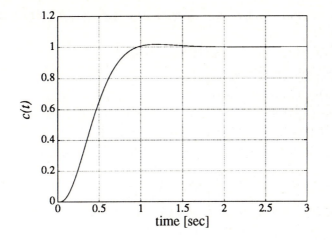

Figure 9.6 Step Response for the Automatic Test System.

characteristic equation, Eq. (9.7), is

$$1 + KK_3 \frac{s^2 + 8s + 20}{s(s+1)(s+5)} = 0.$$

The selected gain, $KK_3 = 12$, lies in the performance region, as shown in Figure 9.5. The **rlocfind** function is used to determine the value of KK_3 at the selected point. The final gains are

$$
\begin{aligned}
K &= 240.00 \\
K_1 &= 1.00 \\
K_2 &= 0.35 \\
K_3 &= 0.05
\end{aligned}
$$

The controller design results in a settling time of about 1.8 seconds and an overshoot of 3%, as shown in Figure 9.6.

9.4 Time Response

The time response of the system in Eq. (9.1) is given by the solution to the vector differential equation

$$\boldsymbol{x}(t) = \exp(\boldsymbol{A}t)\boldsymbol{x}(0) + \int_0^t \exp[\boldsymbol{A}(t-\tau)]\boldsymbol{B}u(\tau)d\tau. \tag{9.8}$$

The matrix exponential function in Eq. (9.8) is the state transition matrix, $\phi(t)$, where

$$\phi(t) = \exp(At).$$

We can use the function **expm** to compute the transition matrix for a given delta time, as illustrated in Figure 9.7. The **expm(A)** function computes the matrix exponential whereas the **exp(A)** function returns $e^{a_{ij}}$ for each of the elements $a_{ij} \in A$.

The time response of the system in Eq. (9.1) can be obtained by using the **lsim** function. The **lsim** function can accept as input nonzero initial conditions as well as an input function. This is illustrated in Figure 9.8 for the RLC network (see *MCS, Chapter 9*) described by the state-space representation

$$A = \begin{bmatrix} 0 & -2 \\ 1 & -3 \end{bmatrix}, \quad B = \begin{bmatrix} 2 \\ 0 \end{bmatrix}, \quad D = \begin{bmatrix} 1 & 0 \end{bmatrix}, \text{and } H = 0.$$

The initial conditions are $x_1(0) = x_2(0) = 1$ and the input $u(t) = 0$. If we can compare the results obtained by the **lsim** function and by multiplying the initial condition state vector by the state transition matrix, we find exactly the identical results. At $t = 0.2$ the state transition matrix is given in Figure 9.7. The state at $t = 0.2$ is predicted by the state transition methods to be

$$\begin{pmatrix} x_1 \\ x_2 \end{pmatrix}_{t=0.2} = \begin{bmatrix} 0.9671 & -0.2968 \\ 0.1484 & 0.5219 \end{bmatrix} \begin{pmatrix} x_1 \\ x_2 \end{pmatrix}_{t=0} = \begin{pmatrix} 0.6703 \\ 0.6703 \end{pmatrix}.$$

The state at $t = 0.2$ is also predicted with the **lsim** function to be $x_1(0.2) = x_2(0.2) = 0.6703$.

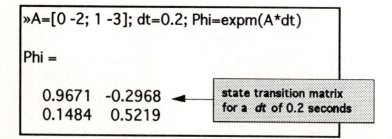

```
»A=[0 -2; 1 -3]; dt=0.2; Phi=expm(A*dt)

Phi =

    0.9671   -0.2968
    0.1484    0.5219
```

state transition matrix for a *dt* of 0.2 seconds

Figure 9.7 Computing the State Transition Matrix for a Given Delta Time.

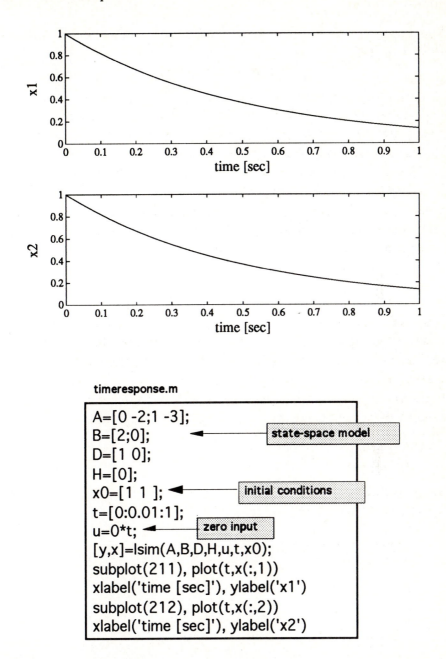

Figure 9.8 Computing the Time Response for Nonzero Initial Conditions and Zero Input.

——————————————— Notes ———————————————

Chapter 10

Control System Design

10.1 Introduction

It is often possible to achieve stability and meet all the control system performance specifications by adjusting one or two parameters. We introduced many examples in the previous chapters illustrating design by adjusting a few parameters. However, in many cases it is necessary to add a *dynamic compensator* into the system. Altering a control system to meet relative stability and performance specifications is called *compensation*. We say that our compensators are dynamic in the sense that the compensator is itself a system described by a transfer function or state-space representation with internal states. A compensator is shown in the control system in Figure 10.1. The compensator in Figure 10.1 is a *cascade* or series

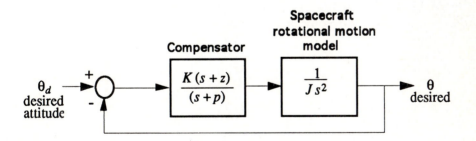

Figure 10.1 A Compensated Control System for Spacecraft Rotational Motion.

compensator since it is placed in the feedforward path. A compensator placed in the feedback path is known as a *feedback* compensator. Compensators can be placed in other paths (e.g., inner feedback loops) in the control system as well.

The main topic of this chapter is compensation of feedback control systems. There are many approaches to compensation. We will consider lead and lag compensators and present a design example that uses both the root locus method and the Bode frequency-domain method to design the compensators. One of the most commonly used compensators is the proportional plus derivative plus integral (PID). The PID compensator is covered in Chapter 11.

10.2   Lead Compensation

Consider the series compensator

$$G_c(s) = \frac{K(s+z)}{s+p}. \tag{10.1}$$

The selection of the variables K, z, and p is based on satisfying the design performance specifications. Whenever

$$|z| < |p|$$

the compensator in Eq. (10.1) is a *lead* compensator. The pole-zero diagram of the lead compensator is shown in Figure 10.2. We can

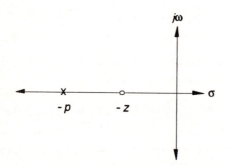

Figure 10.2 Pole-Zero Diagram of the Lead Compensator.

rewrite Eq. (10.1) as

$$G_c(s) = \frac{K(1 + \alpha\tau s)}{\alpha(1 + \tau s)} \qquad (10.2)$$

where $\tau = 1/p$, $\alpha = p/z$ and $\alpha > 1$. The maximum value of the phase lead occurs at a frequency ω_m, where

$$\omega_m = \sqrt{zp} = \frac{1}{\tau\sqrt{\alpha}}.$$

The maximum phase angle at ω_m is ϕ_m, where

$$\sin\phi_m = \frac{\alpha - 1}{\alpha + 1}.$$

Consider, for example, the lead compensator

$$G_c(s) = \frac{10(s + 1)}{s + 10}.$$

The associated Bode diagram is shown in Figure 10.3. The maximum value of the phase lead occurs at

$$\omega_m = \sqrt{zp} = \sqrt{10}.$$

The maximum phase lead is

$$\phi_m = \arcsin(\frac{\alpha - 1}{\alpha + 1}) = 54.9°,$$

where $\alpha = 10$.

The phase-lead compensator is a differentiator type compensator. This can be seen by considering the case when $|p| >> |z|$. Then it follows that

$$G_c(s) \approx [\frac{K}{p}]s.$$

We can design lead compensators with frequency-domain design techniques utilizing Bode diagrams as well as with root locus design methods. The lead compensator increases the phase margin, thus providing additional stability, and increases the system bandwidth to provide speedier dynamic response.

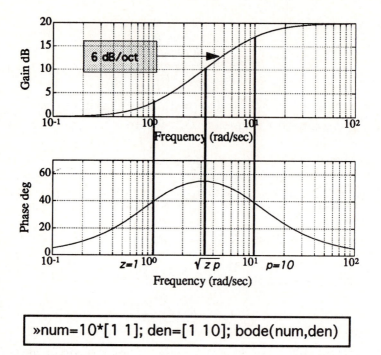

```
»num=10*[1 1]; den=[1 10]; bode(num,den)
```

Figure 10.3 Bode Diagram of the Lead Compensator.

10.3   Lag Compensators

Again consider the series compensator

$$G_c(s) = \frac{K(s+z)}{s+p}.$$

Whenever

$$|p| < |z|$$

the compensator $G_c(s)$ is a *lag* compensator. The pole-zero diagram of the lag compensator is shown in Figure 10.4. The lag compensator can also be written as in Eq. (10.2) where $\alpha < 1$. The maximum value of the phase lag occurs at

$$\omega_m = \sqrt{zp} = \sqrt{10}.$$

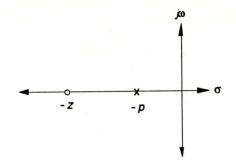

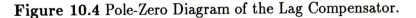

Figure 10.4 Pole-Zero Diagram of the Lag Compensator.

Consider, for example, the lag compensator

$$G_c(s) = \frac{0.1(s+10)}{s+1}.$$

The associated Bode diagram is shown in Figure 10.5.

We see that the lag compensator is an integration type compensator by considering $|z| >> |p|$. Then

$$G_c(s) \approx K + \frac{Kz}{s}.$$

This has the same form as the widely used lag compensator

$$G_c(s) = K_p + \frac{K_I}{s}.$$

This is known as a proportional plus integral (PI) compensator.

The lag compensator is applicable when high steady-state accuracy is required. Although it is possible to increase steady-state accuracy by simply increasing the system gain, this often leads to unacceptable transient response and sometimes instability. This problem is overcome with the addition of a lag compensator and properly chosen values of K, p, and z. The lag compensator decreases the system bandwidth thus suppressing high frequency noise and slows down the transient response.

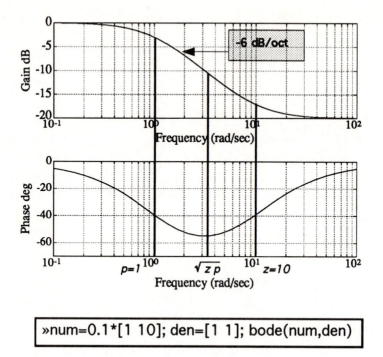

»num=0.1*[1 10]; den=[1 1]; bode(num,den)

Figure 10.5 Bode Diagram of the Lag Compensator.

10.4   Example: Rotor Winder Control System

The rotor winder control system is shown in Figure 10.6 (see *MCS, pp. 542-545*). The design objective is to achieve high steady-state accuracy to a ramp input. The steady-state error to a unit ramp

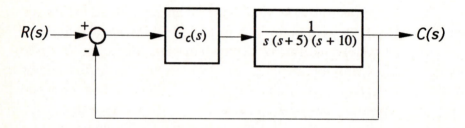

Figure 10.6 Rotor Winder Control System.

input, $R(s) = 1/s^2$, is

$$e_{ss} = \frac{1}{K_v},$$

where

$$K_v = \lim_{s \to 0} \frac{G_c(s)}{50}.$$

Of course, the performance specification of overshoot and settling time must be considered as well as steady-state tracking error. In all likelihood, a simple gain will not be satisfactory. So we will consider active compensation utilizing lead and lag compensators using both Bode diagrams and root locus plots. Our approach is to develop a series of scripts to aid in the compensator designs.

Consider first a simple gain controller, $G_c(s)$, where

$$G_c(s) = K.$$

Then,

$$e_{ss} = \frac{50}{K}.$$

Clearly, the larger we make K, the smaller the steady-state error e_{ss}. However, we must consider the effects of increasing K on the transient response. This is shown in Figure 10.7. When $K = 500$, our steady-state error for a ramp is 10% but the overshoot is 70% and the settling time is around 8 seconds for a step input. We consider this to be unacceptable performance and turn to compensation. The two important compensator types that we consider are lead and lag compensators.

First we try a lead compensator

$$G_c(s) = \frac{K(s + z)}{(s + p)},$$

where $|z| < |p|$. The lead compensator will give us the capability to improve the transient response. We will use a frequency domain approach to design the lead compensator.

Suppose we desire a steady-state error of less than 10% to a ramp input. Then we desire

$$K_v = 10.$$

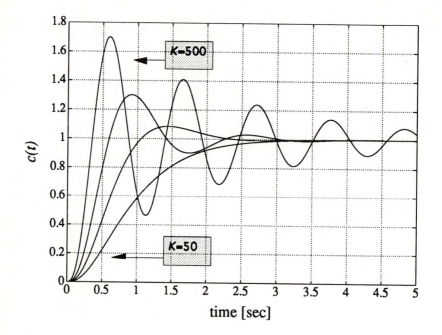

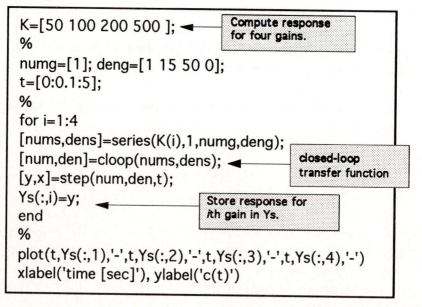

rotorgain.m

```
K=[50 100 200 500 ];          Compute response
%                              for four gains.
numg=[1]; deng=[1 15 50 0];
t=[0:0.1:5];
%
for i=1:4
[nums,dens]=series(K(i),1,numg,deng);
[num,den]=cloop(nums,dens);        closed-loop
[y,x]=step(num,den,t);             transfer function
Ys(:,i)=y;          Store response for
end                 ith gain in Ys.
%
plot(t,Ys(:,1),'-',t,Ys(:,2),'-',t,Ys(:,3),'-',t,Ys(:,4),'-')
xlabel('time [sec]'), ylabel('c(t)')
```

Figure 10.7 Transient Response for Simple Gain Controller.

In addition to the steady-state specifications, suppose also that we desire to meet certain performance specifications:

(i) settling time $T_s \leq 3$ seconds, and

(ii) percent overshoot for a step input $\leq 10\%$.

Solving the approximate formulas

$$P.O. \approx 100 \exp^{-\zeta\pi/\sqrt{1-\zeta^2}} = 10 \quad \text{and} \quad T_s \approx \frac{4}{\zeta\omega_n} = 3$$

for ζ and ω_n yields

$$\zeta = 0.5912 \quad \text{and} \quad \omega_n = 2.2555.$$

The phase margin requirement becomes

$$\phi_{pm} \approx \frac{\zeta}{0.01} = 60 \text{ degrees.}$$

The steps leading to the final design are as follows:

1. Obtain the uncompensated system Bode diagram with $K = 500$ and compute the phase margin.

2. Determine the amount of necessary phase lead.

3. Evaluate α where $\sin \phi_m = \frac{\alpha-1}{\alpha+1}$.

4. Compute $10 \log \alpha$ and find the frequency ω_m on the uncompensated Bode diagram where the magnitude curve is equal to $-10 \log \alpha$.

5. In the neighborhood around ω_m on the uncompensated Bode, draw a line through the 0-dB point at ω_m with slope equal to the current slope plus 20 dB/dec. Locate the intersection of the line with the uncompensated Bode to determine the lead compensation zero location. Then calculate the lead compensator pole location as $p = \alpha z$.

6. Draw the compensated Bode and check the phase margin. Repeat any steps if necessary.

7. Raise the gain to account for attenuation $(1/\alpha)$.

8. Verify the final design with simulation using step functions, and repeat any steps if necessary.

We utilize three scripts in the design. The design scripts are shown in Figures 10.8, 10.9, and 10.10. The first script is for the uncompensated Bode, the next is for the compensated Bode, and the final script is for the step response analysis. The final lead compensator design is

$$G_c(s) = \frac{1800(s + 3.5)}{(s + 25)}.$$

The settling time and overshoot specifications are satisfied, but $K_v = 5$, resulting in a 20% steady-state error to a ramp input. It is possible to continue the design iteration and refine the compensator somewhat, although it should be clear that the lead compensator has added phase margin and improved the transient response as anticipated.

To improve the steady-state errors we can consider the lag compensator. The lag compensator has the form

$$G_c(s) = \frac{K(s + z)}{(s + p)},$$

where $|p| < |z|$. We will use a root locus approach to design the lag compensator, although it can be done using Bode as well. The desired root location region of the dominant roots are specified by

$$\zeta = 0.5912 \quad \text{and} \quad \omega_n = 2.2555.$$

The steps in the design are as follows:

1. Obtain the root locus of the uncompensated system.

2. Locate suitable root locations on the uncompensated system which lie in the region defined by $\zeta = 0.5912$ and $\omega_n = 2.2555$.

3. Calculate the loop gain at the desired root location and the system error constant, $K_{v_{uncomp}}$.

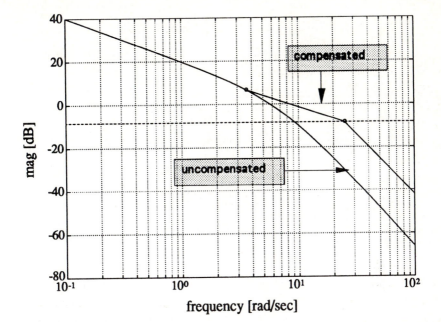

rotorlead.m

```
K=500;  numg=[1]; deng=[1 15 50 0];
[num,den]=series(K,1,numg,deng);        Compute phase margin.
w=logspace(-1,2,200);
[mag,phase,w]=bode(num,den,w);
[Gm,Pm,Wcg,Wcp]=margin(mag,phase,w);
%
Phi=(60-Pm)*pi/180;              additional phase lead
%
alpha=(1+sin(Phi))/(1-sin(Phi))        Compute α.
%
M=-10*log10(alpha)*ones(length(w),1);
%                                       Plot -10 log(α) line to
                                        aid in locating ωm.
[mag,phase,w]=bode(num,den,w);
semilogx(w,20*log10(mag),w,M), grid
xlabel('frequency [rad/sec]'), ylabel('mag [dB]')
```

Figure 10.8 Lead Compensator: Uncompensated Bode.

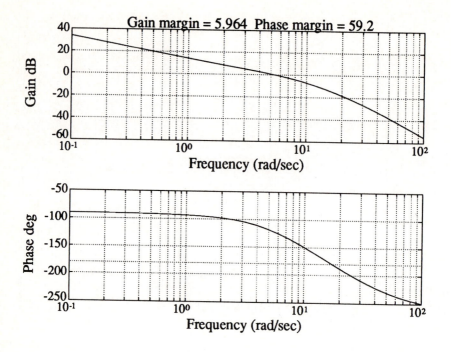

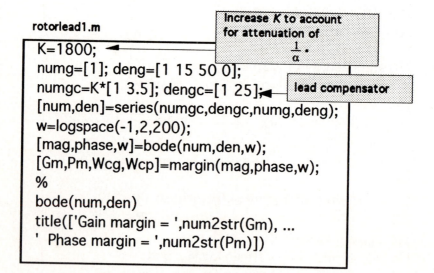

Figure 10.9 Lead Compensator: Compensated Bode.

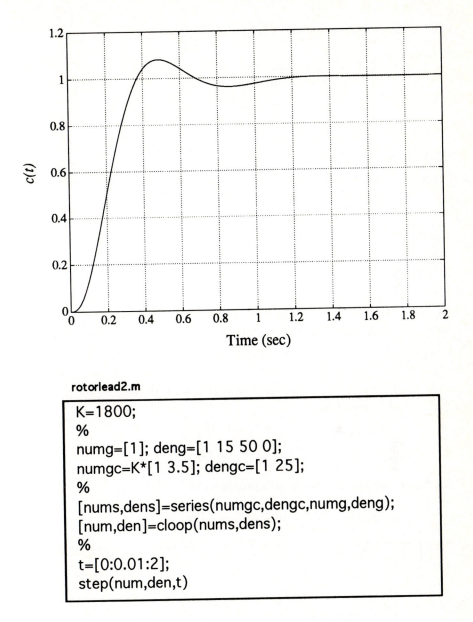

rotorlead2.m

```
K=1800;
%
numg=[1]; deng=[1 15 50 0];
numgc=K*[1 3.5]; dengc=[1 25];
%
[nums,dens]=series(numgc,dengc,numg,deng);
[num,den]=cloop(nums,dens);
%
t=[0:0.01:2];
step(num,den,t)
```

Figure 10.10 Lead Compensator: Step Response.

4. Compute $\alpha = \frac{K_{vcomp}}{K_{vuncomp}}$ where $K_{vcomp} = 10$.

5. With α known, determine suitable locations of the compensator pole and zero so that the compensated root locus still passes through desired location.

6. Verify with simulation and repeat any steps if necessary.

The design methodology is shown in Figures 10.11, 10.12, and 10.13. Using the **rlocfind** function, we can compute the gain K associated with the roots of our choice on the uncompensated root locus that lie in the performance region. We then compute α to ensure that we achieve the desired K_v. We place the lag compensator pole and zero in order not to impact the uncompensated root locus. In Figure 10.12, the lag compensator pole and zero are very near the origin at $z = -0.1$ and $p = -0.01$.

The settling time and overshoot specifications are nearly satisfied and $K_v = 10$ as desired. It is possible to continue the design iteration and refine the compensator somewhat, although it should be clear that the lag compensator has improved the steady-state errors to a ramp input relative to the lead compensator design. The final lag compensator design is

$$G_c(s) = \frac{100(s + 0.1)}{(s + 0.01)}.$$

The resulting performance is summarized in Table 10.1.

Table 10.1 Compensator Design Results.

Controller	Gain, K	Lead	Lag
Step overshoot	70%	8%	13%
Settling time (sec)	8	1	4
Steady-state error for ramp	10%	20%	10%
K_v	10	5	10

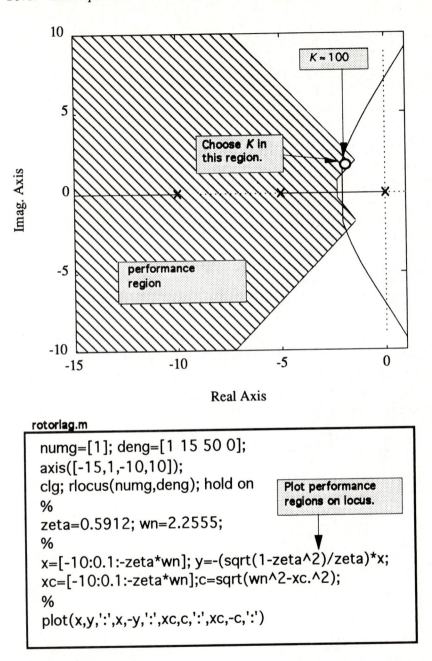

Figure 10.11 Lag Compensator: Uncompensated Root Locus.

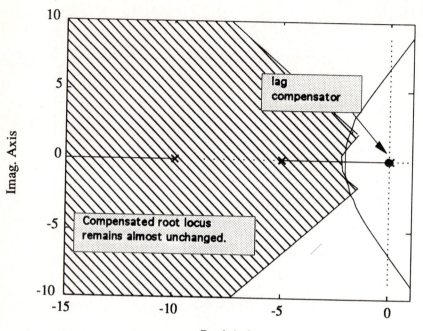

rotorlag1.m

```
numg=[1]; deng=[1 15 50 0];
numgc=[1 0.1]; dengc=[1 0.01];
[num,den]=series(numgc,dengc,numg,deng);
axis([-15,1,-10,10]);
clg; rlocus(num,den); hold on
%
zeta=0.5912; wn=2.2555;
x=[-10:0.1:-zeta*wn]; y=-(sqrt(1-zeta^2)/zeta)*x;
xc=[-10:0.1:-zeta*wn];c=sqrt(wn^2-xc.^2);
plot(x,y,':',x,-y,':',xc,c,':',xc,-c,':')
```

Figure 10.12 Lag Compensator: Compensated Root Locus.

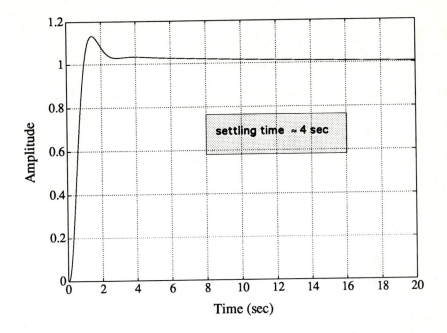

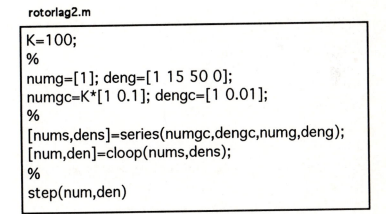

rotorlag2.m

```
K=100;
%
numg=[1]; deng=[1 15 50 0];
numgc=K*[1 0.1]; dengc=[1 0.01];
%
[nums,dens]=series(numgc,dengc,numg,deng);
[num,den]=cloop(nums,dens);
%
step(num,den)
```

Figure 10.13 Lag Compensator: Step Response.

——————————— Notes ———————————

Chapter 11

Robust Control Systems

11.1 Introduction

Designing a highly accurate control system in the presence of plant uncertainty is a classical design problem. In the previous chapters, we have generally assumed that the plant parameters are well known and designed our control system accordingly. In practice, the plant parameters are never precisely known and may vary slowly over time. It is desirable to design a control system that performs adequately over a range of plant parameters. A control system is *robust* when it maintains a satisfactory level of stability and performance over a range of plant parameters and disturbances.

In this chapter, we begin to investigate robust control systems. In particular we consider the commonly used proportional plus deriva-

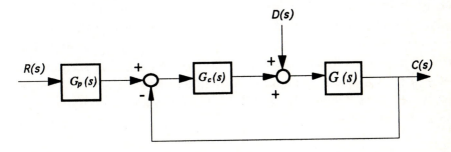

Figure 11.1 Feedback Control System with Reference and Disturbance Inputs and a Prefilter.

151

tive plus integral (PID) controller. Our feedback control system has the form shown in Figure 11.1. Notice that the system has a *prefilter* $G_p(s)$. The role of the prefilter in contributing to optimum performance is discussed in *MCS, pp. 594-595.*

11.2   Robust PID Controlled Systems

The PID controller has the form

$$G_c(s) = \frac{K_3 s^2 + K_1 s + K_2}{s}.$$

Notice that the PID controller is not a rational function (i.e., the degree of the numerator polynomial is greater than the degree of the denominator polynomial). You will experience difficulty if you attempt to input the PID controller into *MATLAB* in the standard numerator and denominator fashion. Generally speaking, the problem can be resolved by utilizing the **conv** function rather than the **series** function in your manipulations.

The objective is to choose the parameters K_1, K_2, and K_3 to meet the performance specifications and have desirable robustness properties. Unfortunately, it is not immediately clear how to choose the parameters in the PID controller to obtain certain robustness characteristics. We will show by an illustrative example that it is possible to choose the parameters iteratively and verify the robustness by simulation. Using *MATLAB* helps in this process since the entire design and simulation can be mechanized utilizing scripts and easily executed again and again. A complete exposition on the subject of robust control analysis and design is beyond the scope of this book.

■ EXAMPLE 11.1 Robust Control of Temperature

Consider the feedback control system in Figure 11.1, where

$$G(s) = \frac{1}{(s + c_0)^2}$$

and the nominal value of c_0 is

$$c_0 = 1.$$

We will design a compensator based on $c_0 = 1$ and check robustness by simulation. Our design specifications are as follows:

(i) settling time $T_s \leq 0.5$ seconds, and

(ii) optimum ITAE performance for a step input (see *MCS, pp. 176-185*).

In our design, we will not utilize a prefilter to meet specification (ii) but will instead show that acceptable performance (i.e., low overshoot) can be obtained by increasing the system gain.
The closed-loop transfer function is

$$T(s) = \frac{K_3 s^2 + K_1 s + K_2}{s^3 + (2 + K_3)s^2 + (1 + K_1)s + K_2}. \tag{11.1}$$

The associated characteristic equation is

$$1 + K^*(\frac{s^2 + as + b}{s^3}) = 0,$$

where

$$K^* = K_3 + 2,$$

$$a = \frac{1 + K_1}{2 + K_3},$$

$$b = \frac{K_2}{2 + K_3}.$$

Our settling time requirement $T_s < \frac{1}{2}$ leads us to choose the roots of $s^2 + as + b$ to the left of the $s = -\zeta \omega_n = -8$ line in the s-plane, as shown in Figure 11.2, to ensure that the locus travels into the required performance region. We have chosen $a = 16$ and $b = 70$ to ensure the locus travels past the $s = -8$ line. We select a point on the root locus in the performance region, and using the **rlocfind** function, we find the associated gain K^* and the associated value of

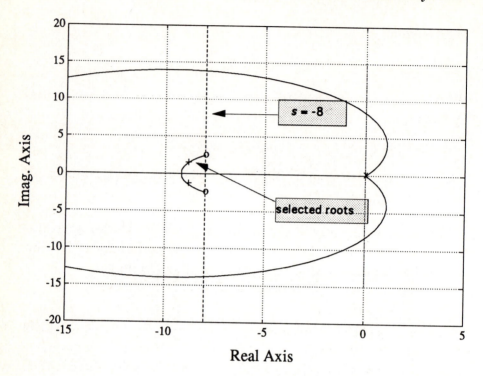

Figure 11.2 Root Locus for the PID Compensated Temperature Controller.

ω_n. For the point we have chosen we find that

$$K^* = 118.$$

Then, with K^*, a, and b we can solve for the PID coefficients as follows:

$$K_3 = K^* - 2 = 116,$$

$$K_1 = a(2 + K_3) - 1 = 1187,$$

$$K_2 = b(2 + K3) = 8260.$$

To meet the overshoot performance requirements for a step input we will utilize a cascade gain K that will be chosen by iterative methods using the **step** function. This is illustrated in Figure 11.3. The step response corresponding to $K = 5$ has an acceptable overshoot of 2%. With the addition of the gain $K = 5$, the final PID controller is

$$G_c(s) = K \; \frac{K_3 s^2 + K_1 s + K_2}{s} = 5 \; \frac{116 s^2 + 1187 s + 8260}{s}. \quad (11.2)$$

We did not used the prefilter as is done in the design Example 11.5 in *MCS, pp. 594-595*. Instead we increased the system gain to obtain satisfactory transient response. Now we can consider the question of robustness to changes in the plant parameter c_0.

Our investigation into the robustness of our design consists of a step response analysis using the PID controller given in Eq. (11.2) for a range of plant parameter variations of $c_0 \in [0.1, 10]$. The results are displayed in Figure 11.4. The script is written to compute the step response for a given c_0. It might be a good idea to place the input of c_0 at the command prompt level to make the script more interactive.

The simulation results indicate that the PID design is robust with respect to changes in c_0. The differences in the step responses for $c_0 \in [0.1, 10]$ are barely discernible on the plot. If the results showed otherwise, it would be possible to iterate on the design until an acceptable performance was achieved.

There exist various control design methods that incorporate robustness directly into the design process, but their presentation here is outside the scope of this text. The interactive capability of *MATLAB* allows us to check our robustness by simulation, although this is clearly not the most desirable approach to design.

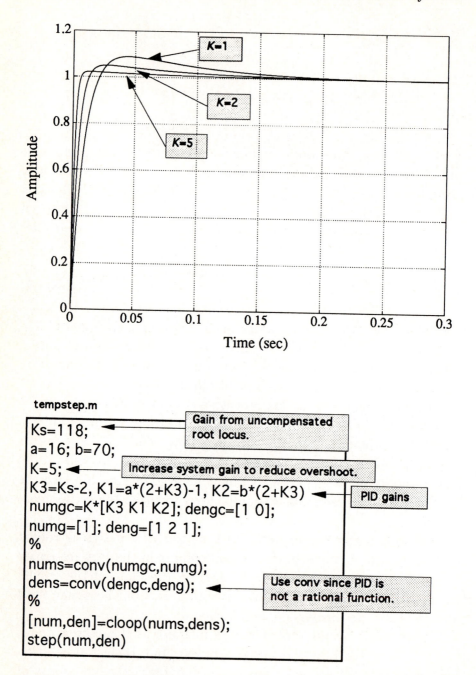

Figure 11.3 Step Response for the PID Temperature Controller.

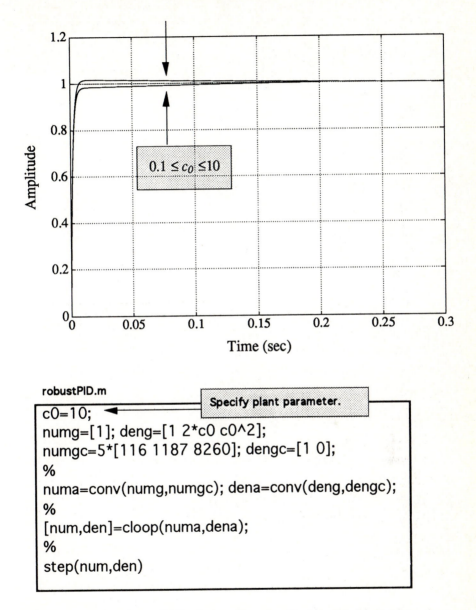

Figure 11.4 Robust PID Controller Analysis with Variations in c_0.

——————————————— Notes ———————————————

Index/Glossary

axis Controls the manual axis scaling on plots; 105

bode Computes a Bode frequency response plot; 92-93, 107, 110, 122

clear Removes variables and functions from memory; 6, 9
clg Clears plots from the graph window; 16
cloop Computes the closed-loop system with unity feedback; 26, 37-40, 122
conv Multiplies two polynomials via convolution; 26, 31-32, 152

end Terminates a **for** function; 75
expm Computes the matrix exponential function; 130

feedback Computes the feedback interconnection of two systems; 26, 37-40, 49, 122
for Repeats a group of statements a specific number of times; 71, 75

format Controls the output format; 9

grid Draws grid lines on the current plot; 17

help Invokes the help facility; 22

impulse Computes the unit impulse response of a system; 61, 63, 122

loglog Generates an x-y plot using log-log scales; 17-18, 20
logspace Generates a logarithmically spaced frequency vector for frequency response analysis; 92-95
lsim Computes the time response of a system to an arbitrary input and initial conditions; 61, 66, 68, 122, 130

margin Computes the gain margin, phase margin, and associated crossover frequencies from frequency response data; 103, 107-110

159

subplot Subdivides the graph display into sub-windows; 17, 20

tfss Converts a transfer function system representation to a state-space representation; 122-123

title Puts a title on the current plot; 17

who Lists the variables in the workspace; 7, 9-10

whos Lists the variables in the workspace including their size and type; 7, 9

xlabel Puts an x-axis label on the current plot; 17

ylabel Puts a y-axis label on the current plot; 17

The
MATH
WORKS
Inc.

Bishop

BUSINESS REPLY MAIL

FIRST CLASS   PERMIT NO. 82   NATICK, MA

POSTAGE WILL BE PAID BY ADDRESSEE

THE MATHWORKS, INC.
24 Prime Park Way
Natick, MA 01760-9889